SECRETS
TO SUCCESS
IN SPORT
& PLAY

A street athlete at age six and a national participant at sixteen, Marianne Torbert has played, studied play, and taught kinesiology for several years. She holds a Ph.D. from the University of Southern California and is a faculty member at Temple University. She is the author of another Spectrum book entitled *Follow Me: A Handbook of Movement Activities for Children.*

PRENTICE-HALL INTERNATIONAL, INC., *London*
PRENTICE-HALL OF AUSTRALIA PTY. LIMITED, *Sydney*
PRENTICE-HALL OF CANADA, LTD., *Toronto*
PRENTICE-HALL OF INDIA PRIVATE LIMITED, *New Delhi*
PRENTICE-HALL OF JAPAN, INC., *Tokyo*
PRENTICE-HALL OF SOUTHEAST ASIA PTE. LTD., *Singapore*
WHITEHALL BOOKS LIMITED, *Wellington, New Zealand*

marianne torbert

SECRETS TO SUCCESS IN SPORT & PLAY

A Guide for Players of All Ages

A SPECTRUM BOOK

Prentice-Hall, Inc., Englewood Cliffs, New Jersey 07632

Library of Congress Cataloging in Publication Data

TORBERT, MARIANNE.
   Secrets to success in sport & play.

   "A Spectrum Book."
   Includes index.
     1. Physical education and training.
2. Human mechanics.   3. Motor learning.
I. Title.
GV341.T64   613.7'07   81-19887
                         AACR2

ISBN 0-13-798728-5

ISBN 0-13-798710-2 {PBK.}

Editorial/production supervision by Carol Smith
Cover design by Jeannette Jacobs
Interior illustrations by Doug Parise
Manufacturing buyer: Cathie Lenard

To the many who love
the joy and celebration
of sport and play as players,
teachers, coaches, parents, and spectators.

It is my hope that this book
will allow each reader to enjoy
additional involvement, growth, and skill.

Contents

Foreword

This book is the second of what I hope will be a series by Marianne Torbert. In attempting to write a book of this kind, the author was faced with an unenviable task. There are already countless "how-to" books dealing with the mechanics of sport and games. Unfortunately, many of them contain misconceptions based upon either the folklore of sport or the unsubstantiated opinions of popular sport figures. In reality, an understanding of the mechanics of skilled human movement requires a sound insight into the concepts of Newtonian physics, and some familiarity with the anatomical structure of the body. Thus the information which the author attempted to convey must be scientifically unambiguous, and at times complex. Nevertheless, the book is designed to have wide appeal, and it must be assumed that the typical reader will be unfamiliar with the jargon of science. Therefore the most formidable task in writing this book was to take each separate concept and present it in a manner which would be readily comprehensible to the nonspecialized reader. However, it was also necessary to ensure that the significance of the concept was not lost through over-simplification.

Clearly, Dr. Torbert has succeeded in this most difficult task. The book is dedicated, "to the many who love the joy and celebration of sport and play" and the reader senses that the author shares that love. Her informal writing style and her personal anecdotes are both refreshing and appropriate for the intended readers. The material covered has been carefully chosen to cover a wide variety of sport and play situations. Finally, the book is structured so as to promote learning through participation, rather than by reading alone. These characteristics are the hallmarks of a real educator.

Marianne Torbert's book is highly recommended for players of all ages; for parents, teachers, and coaches of young children; and for students of elementary education. Without a doubt, many readers will search through this delightful little book in the hope of finding the secrets to success in sport and play, and they will indeed uncover those secrets. But, in the search they will also find some of the joys and the magic of science. Perhaps this is the author's greatest gift to her readers.

Peter R. Francis
Past Chairperson
Kinesiology Academy of the American Alliance
of Health, Physical Education, Recreation and Dance

Preface

While teaching people to play I have frequently found that participants as well as some coaches really have no idea about why things happen. There seemed to be a great deal of interest, however, when I would attempt to clarify and simplify the mechanical principles of movement that had so excited me as I had discovered them in various texts. As I fumbled in my attempts to explain certain principles, I found I was learning a great deal myself. A desire to simplify led me to seek help in kinesiology books, and what I found excited me even further.

Although I had been a nationally ranked participant I was now discovering secrets to success in sport and play that I had been unaware of. It was challenging to try out new possibilities and conquer old unsolved problems. My friends and students were assuring me that the application of mechanical principles was working for them in exciting ways too. They were beginning to be able to transfer their understanding from one activity to another. They were more able to help others, whether this was in Little League, weekend golfing, varsity athletics, or working with the children on the playground who seemed destined for the painful syndrome of always being picked last.

As time went on I found myself sharing what I had learned with more and more people until the contents of this book actually evolved; I am presently using it in basic movement workshops that I teach. A friend and respected colleague and author, Dr. Tom Evaul, suggested that the material should be published, which is how *Secrets to Success in Sport & Play* was born. It has gone through the normal labor pains as decisions of inclusion, omission, and format had to be made. My usual but unbelievable luck gave me help from Mr. Peter Francis of the University of Oregon, chairperson of the Academy of Kinesiology of the American Alliance of Health, Physical Education, Recreation and Dance in maintaining scientific honesty in my attempts to simplify and explain materials that frequently involve a somewhat sophisticated understanding of math, engineering, and physics. On occasion I had to admit defeat, and omit an interesting point or exciting venture; I leave them for those of you whose curiosity will commit you to further involvement and investigation in the world of biomechanics and kinesiology.

My personal reason for publishing this work is my desire to share the joy I have known in successful participation in sport and play and the challenge of overcoming the difficult within a partnership of the physical and the mental.

ACKNOWLEDGMENTS

Thanks to:

• Peter R. Francis of the University of Oregon, for his patient and careful assistance in trying to keep me scientifically honest. Any errors in judgment are strictly mine and probably the result of my bullheadedness.

- Dr. Tom Evaul of Temple University, who encouraged me to put this work into book form.

- My students, who helped me to understand Kahlil Gibran's statement: "Thought is a bird of space, that in a cage of words may indeed unfold its wings but cannot fly."

- Doug Parise, whose knowledge of movement, artistic talent, and personal patience and perseverance made the illustrations in this book possible.

- Sharon Denny, whose teaching assistance helped me to survive the final semester in which the manuscript was completed.

- Marie Ray, whose brownies and chocolate chip cookies were a source of needed energy.

- Lynne Lumsden, Editor-in-Chief, Spectrum Books, for her continuous support.

- Prentice-Hall, Inc., whose staff always amazes me with their positive responses to my multiple requests and inquiries. They include Frank Moorman, Debra Leitner, Don Chanfrau, and Dean Karrel.

- Chuck Longnecker and the other members of the Instructional Media Center, College of Health, Physical Education, Recreation and Dance, Temple University, for helping me to capsulize some difficult conceptual material.

- My friends, who are very important—because they are my friends.

- The Cleveland Women's Physical Education Association, which gave its first scholarship to a scared, five-foot-two, one-hundred-pounder, who held a dream of becoming a physical education teacher. That dream came true.

SECRETS TO SUCCESS IN SPORT & PLAY

Introduction

Play has an expanding and unlimited potential to contribute to personal growth. To increase one's understanding of any aspect of play is to increase the personal challenge to be found within it. This challenge can re-create our involvement in life as it produces and increases physical skills that contribute to the quality of our lives by adding to the thrill of playing and at the same time reducing daily accidents, opening doors to social interaction with others, and perhaps increasing our personal confidence.

This book can help you do all of this. I have selected several principles of movement and attempted to incorporate them in a way that will clarify how you can apply them and make them work for you. Did you know that

1. No one is destined to be unskilled.
2. Understanding the keys to the mechanics of sport and play can greatly increase your success; at the same time it can reduce the time normally required to improve your skills.

3. All individuals can improve their balance. By increasing your balance not only your agility but also your power and accuracy will improve.
4. Knowledge of spins can increase your score in many sports, including basketball, tennis, and golf.
5. Understanding some of the basic mechanics of movement could help you begin to become an outstanding coach or player.

The Secrets to Success in Sport and Play was written to assist both those who are seeking personal help and those who wish to help others. The format, which is meant to be participatory, was selected to maximize your sense of involvement. You will find suggestions, observations, experiments, and applications that you might like to try as you read. And if you are interested in more activities to improve the skills described here you can find them in my earlier book, *Follow Me: A Handbook of Movement Activities for Children* (Englewood Cliffs, N.J.: Prentice-Hall, Inc., 1980). I believe you will find that the excitement of participation will increase as you begin to discover the secrets to success in sport and play.

part one

APPROACHING MOVEMENT ANALYSIS

chapter one

Teaching and learning

DEFINING YOUR GOALS

Before you begin, here are three things to keep in mind.

1. Remember that feelings are important to learning and changing.
2. Don't invest your identity in instant success. Mistakes are also a vital part of learning.
3. Try to recognize improvement—even when it may seem minimal.

The Specific Objective Method. Determine your *Objective.* What do you wish to accomplish? Restate this in terms of *needs.* Perhaps you want the tennis ball to go over the net. This is certainly an important goal, but you must become more specific. It would be possible to detail and study all the mechanical principles involved in accomplishing this task, but it would be a great deal quicker and more helpful if you analyzed the specific need you are going to deal with first and directed your efforts toward this goal. For example, if you're not making contact with the ball, perhaps the problem lies in your inability to evaluate visually a moving object (see chapter 9). If you contact the ball but it just doesn't go far enough, you have a force problem and could use the mechanical principles in chapter 4 as a checklist. If you find force improving but now the ball is not going over the net because the hits go wild, then the mechanical principles related to direction and accuracy described in chapter 8 should be most helpful.

Try to enjoy puzzling out what the needs may be for your selected goal. This book should give you an excellent repertoire of possible solutions.

The Correcting Errors Method. The correcting errors approach assumes that a player has become consistent enough to be having a specific problem and is willing to make a concerted effort to correct errors while improving basic skills. The specific error that may be affecting success can be tackled through analysis.

Many players lose their *playfulness* when it comes to making mistakes, and they put a great deal of their energy into suppressing or exhausting their emotions. Perhaps you could be a mental "detective" and make this part of the fun of play. "When things go wrong and they oft times will" it might be better to make a challenge out of finding possible solutions rather than to become angry or discouraged. Here is one method that you might like to try.

- State the problem. Deal with only one problem at a time.

- Skim the table of contents and chapters of this book and jot down any ideas and principles that might be related to the problem in any way. These are possible causes.

- You may find that you are now really warmed up to some possibilities. With this preparation you can begin to zero in on the key to the solution. The way to do this is by using "the curious child" technique (*why, why, why?*). Begin by asking why the problem occurred. Then when you have an answer you may wish to ask why *this* cause occurred. Try to utilize the possibilities you have jotted down, or perhaps find new possibilities you have overlooked.

You may feel a little foolish asking "why" again in relation to your new cause, but the real key to the solution just may be deeper than you realize. Perseverance does pay off. If you work through to the real key the solution will prove a great deal easier and will help to remedy other problems along the way.

A very important factor will be to find the error that occurred first, since that error probably caused other errors to occur later. When you solve the earliest occurring error the errors that followed will tend to correct themselves. But if you only get back to one of the later errors (which is really only an effect or result of the initial error) the initial error will not be corrected, and thus the primary problem will still exist.

Be aware that most movements have three phases:

1. *Preparatory Phase:* backswing, stabilization, weight transfer away from final direction of action, stretching muscles to be involved in action phase
2. *Action Phase:* motion or effort that follows the preparatory phase and precedes the final follow-through phase
3. *Follow-through Phase:* completion of a movement after the action phase; absorption of force; reaching out after a hit, throw, or kick. This may lead into a new preparatory stage, for instance, when catching a throw you rock backward to absorb the force.

Errors can occur during any of these phases, but because the first error may be the cause of all errors that follow it is important to analyze these three phases in their time sequence.

When you feel you have really exhausted the "whys" we will assume that you have found the key to the solution and can move on to the final steps.

• Attempt to put your solution into practice. Be patient. Remember, correcting an error takes time. It may be more difficult than other forms of learning because you may also be working on breaking habits.

• Finally, practice your observational skills. You can learn a great deal from both good and bad players. Can you determine why the former succeed and why the latter fail?

ENCOURAGING THE LEARNER

• A visual model gives learners an idea of what they are supposed to be doing. This can be a demonstration, a loop film, a picture, or observation of a live or televised performance. I have noted that learners tend to focus on the results rather than concentrating on the action phase of the motion, so I no longer demonstrate by hitting a ball *over* the net or shooting a ball *into* the basket. I have found that learners retain more of the relevant aspects of the demonstration when the result becomes irrelevant.

• Remember that young children tend to be nonverbal. Try to help them understand through *experiencing*. Games and movement activities can be selected that will enable them to practice specific foundation skills. These foundation skills (balance, visual tracking, absorbing force, changing directions, stopping and starting, spatial awareness, and reading movement) are vital since they underlie many activity skills.

The activities and games should also allow for extensive participation in good, fun practice to reinforce important basic skills.

• Try to have a thorough understanding of the mechanical principles involved so that your help can be specific and keyed to the particular skill or problem involved.

• Avoid giving too much information at once. Solve only one problem at a time. Focus on keys. These will be given throughout the chapters that follow.

• Try to develop special key words and phrases that seem to be helpful and are understood by as many as possible. The "gorilla" principle in chapter 3 is an example.

• Be patient. The tension created by stress is both an emotional and a physical deterrent to learning. It requires time and lots of repetition to compute what works; get the "feeling" for moving (kinesthetic sense); recognize flight and rebound patterns; learn to know what to attend to; time your moves; and let extraneous, ineffective, or overflow movements be extinguished.

• By utilizing the mechanical principles of movement you can see and help others to see relationships, make wise choices and decisions, and increase the possibility of a transfer of learning from one activity or situation to another.

The principles of balance, force production, motion and leverage are identical regardless of the activity.[1]

The purpose of each (movement pattern) causes some adjustments, but the basic mechanics remain the same.[2]

An understanding of principles or procedures underlying the initial task will result in greater transfer to a different activity.[3]

• Try to determine "progressions" for growth. Consider reducing the complexity or the number of problems to be solved at any one time. Try to simplify, perhaps breaking the skill down or utilizing a lead-up activity. Try to reduce the number of things in motion. Use a tee, tether, or trough (Figure 1-1). Use balloons, beach balls, or other slow-moving objects. Toss slowly and accurately to the beginner. Increase the size of the object or striking implements without increasing the weight. And try to make initial experiences consistent, simple, and successful.

[1] Marion R. Broer and Ronald F. Zernicke, *Efficiency of Human Movement* (Philadelphia, Penna.: W. B. Saunders Company, 1979), p. 29.

[2] Ibid., p. 13.

[3] Joseph B. Oxendine, *Psychology of Motor Learning* (New York: Appleton-Century-Crofts, 1968), p. 97.

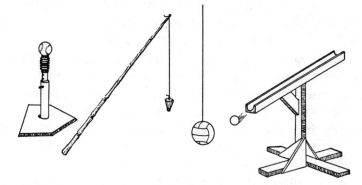

FIGURE 1-1

- Help the players establish obtainable goals and see and feel their successes. Positive feelings about growth and improvement increase motivation and challenge and reduce threat, another deterrent to learning.

- Make sure that each participant has *many* trials, is challenged at his or her level, and has some success.

- Create an environment that supports trying and allows for the errors that normally occur during learning.

- Try to reduce the fears of failure and of injury. Sometimes equipment can be effectively modified. Be creative.

- Until players gain the ability to be forceful, accurate, and move well they may have to compensate—for instance, send the ball high to get it over the net in volleyball, use a lighter ball or bat, or lower the basket. These techniques are helpful during the process of learning and can be modified as abilities develop and improve.

- Try to avoid correcting a player in front of others if this seems to be embarrassing. You might do a role change in which you let the participants (individual or group) find an error that *you* demonstrate. This avoids pointing out who made the error, and it encourages players to become good observers.

- Players may need creative "helps" to sense specific body

positions or develop specific foundation skills. Be inventive. Have fun creating new helps. Remember that we do not all learn in the same way or through the same methods. For example,

1. Use a rope with a knot in the end of it or a streamer of crepe paper to get the feeling of the full reach of an overhead throw or tennis serve.
2. Play catch with plastic milk jug scoops to learn about "giving" to absorb force.
3. Have a beginner reach bank and touch a fence, your hand, or a hanging object to get the feeling of a full backswing.
4. Have players swing bats or rackets along a tennis net or rope to get the feeling of a level swing (not scooping ⟍➤ or dropping the bat or racket ⟍➤).
5. Set up two or three cones (tees), each with a ball on it. Have players hit "through" the balls to get the feeling of a level swing (Figure 1-2).

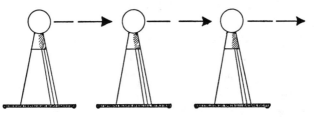

FIGURE 1-2

6. Suspend a paper plate at the proper height and position in relation to the individual and ask the tennis player, who is learning to serve, to ball toss gently and accurately to just touch the plate (Figure 1-3).
7. Have volleyball players "set" the ball through a basketball hoop. This encourages good technique, while providing a built-in motivation—clear and immediate measurement of the degree of success (Figure 1-4, page 13).

• You may want to avoid fighting old habit patterns. Try starting with what is *un*familiar but related. For example, do the backhand in tennis before trying to break the self-taught

FIGURE 1-3

forehand with all its bad habits. Do the backward roll before the forward roll. (Actually the loss of balance that initiates the roll is accomplished more readily in the backward roll.) Later you can relate what was learned to the familiar and hope for positive transfer.

• Be aware of and sensitive to the problems of those who may do things differently: the nearsighted individual, the heavy-set player, the awkward adolescent who is dealing with a changing body, the individual who feels uncomfortable attempting a new skill, the tense individual, the left-handed player, and so

FIGURE 1-4

on. For example, instead of using terms like "left" or "right" consider terms that can apply to both left- and right-handed players, such as "other," "opposite," "net foot," "racket hand," and so on.

• Encourage thinking. Attempt to build a learning progression that will allow for independent learning as players develop in skill and understanding. One possible approach over time might be:

1. Tell beginners how to do something.
2. Later ask participants what you told them.
3. Tell participants why something is done a certain way (mechanical principles of movement). Stay simple.
4. Later ask players why something is done a certain way. (You may be interested in finding out just what they thought you said.)
5. Show beginners similarities between various skills and situations. Encourage generalization and transfer of learning, for instance with the overhand throw and the tennis serve.
6. Guide players to see transfer of similarities between various skills, such as bowling and the underhand throw.
7. Ask players to tell you about similarities between old and new activities.
8. Ask players to relate mechanical principles .to the objective of a particular known skill.
9. Ask participants to relate principles to the objective of an unknown or new skill.
10. Ask players to make decisions about how to do something based upon their "growing" understanding.

Many individuals for one reason or another—fear, initial failure, a rapidly changing body, size, unreal expectations, vision problems, lack of experience at a very basic level, or individual uniqueness—need to and can grow from a good situation that allows for multiple repetitions in a safe and comfortable environment. This may require sensitivity, patience, and creative selection or modification on the part of another.

This type of help can be of tremendous value during any part of an individual's life and may contribute very positively to the pleasure he or she enjoys while playing. I had an interesting experience that taught me that although you do not always directly witness this effect, it may still happen. I was in an elevator in a large office building in Columbus, Ohio. A tall, lanky, young man got on and, looking right at me, said, "Hello,

Ms. Torbert, I'll bet you don't know who I am." His face seemed familiar, but my recall allowed me little more than a vague hunch that this young man's name was Rick. He *was* Rick; the last time I had seen him he was two-thirds as tall and ten to twelve years younger. He had been the awkward, persevering kid who had taken free tennis lessons with me years before. To my surprise he had gone on to do quite well. He knew and had played with nationally ranked tennis players. He had come a long way—a distance I wouldn't have predicted while watching him struggle to get to and hit the ball, trying to deal with his body and the complexity of a bouncing ball a decade earlier. Rick thanked me for the initial start he had received from those early lessons. But as he left and the door closed behind him I realized that he had just given me a bigger gift. He had let me know that the help we give, sometimes wondering if it has been of any value, may reap unseen results. And that potential end is so worth the effort.

part two

MOVING YOURSELF

chapter two

Balance

Balance is the foundation from which we initiate all movement. Without balance many tasks become relatively difficult or even impossible. We cannot effectively develop force nor can we hope for accuracy, consistency, or coordination without good balance. Observe a skillful athlete and it becomes evident that the capability to lose and regain balance is the key to agility (the ability to change directions rapidly), maneuverability, and all other efficient uses of the body. Improving balance increases the degree of control and adaptability athletes have in relation to their movements.

For individuals who do not move well or are considered clumsy balance should be an area of focus and practice. Many individuals spend many embarrassing moments, have more than the average number of injuries, and fail unnecessarily because they have not had sufficiently rich developmental balance experiences. In at least three different periods of life it may become necessary for all of us to learn or redevelop some aspects of this physical skill—toddlerhood; adolescence, when the body may be in a rapid state of change; and as a senior citizen, when some of the physical faculties that we have relied upon for balance may begin to diminish (sight, muscular endurance, strength, flexibility, and the mechanism in the semi-circular canals in the ears).

Because balance can be improved at any age and is of lifetime importance to each person's social, emotional, and physical well-being it becomes important that fun, safe, activities involving balance be selected and their frequent use encouraged. Many times we overlook the additional opportunity to include this type of activity as part of prepractice warm-ups, in family play, at picnics, during periods that could use a shot in the arm, or as a fun conclusion to a practice session. All players, children and adults, need a diet of fun, repetition, noneliminating types of games, lots of practice on specific skills, and opportunities for evaluation and improvement. These are a vital part of the process. Many activities can be found in my book, *Follow Me,* that can help you get started, that can be played by people of any age and any level from the beginner or the player who has balance difficulties to the varsity-level player.

PRINCIPLES OF BALANCE

While balance can be improved through experience and practice, individuals who understand the three mechanical principles that govern balance can help themselves and others by analyzing the causes of specific balance difficulties and making helpful suggestions or decisions that can greatly reduce the amount of trial and error required to increase balance ability. This in turn reduces the injury potential, increases the success ratio, and allows participants to experience success more rapidly. The three important principles of balance are:

1. Keep your weight centered over your base of support.

$$\frac{c \ of \ g}{b \ of \ s}$$

2. Increase the size of your foundation (base of support)—for example, spread your feet.

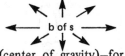

3. Lower your weight (center of gravity)—for example, bend your knees.

The concept of the *center of gravity* is important for those who wish to understand the principles of balance and later the principles related to the human being as a projectile (see Chapter 7). A person's center of gravity is the point around which the body can be balanced. Although it is found roughly in the area behind the umbilicus (belly button) it will vary with body build and change with each new position of the body. Thus if we shift our weight (for instance, raise an arm, putting more body weight above the waist) the center of gravity must also shift in this direction to continue to balance the weight. If we move a leg backward and upward, as in the preparatory backswing for a kick, the center of gravity will also shift backward and upward within the body. These changes frequently require a shift of the body position so that the center of gravity can remain over the base of support for stability.

As the center of gravity moves nearer the outer border of the base of support relative instability occurs. When the center of gravity moves beyond the base of support the body is no longer in balance (stability) and we will have to shift our position to bring the center of gravity back over the base of support or instability, falling, or movement will occur (Figure 2-1).

There are actually two kinds of balance. The first is called *static balance* or minimal movement balance (such as a headstand) in which one attempts to make only slight shifts to keep the center of gravity over the base of support and maintain balance in a relatively still state. The second is *dynamic balance* or moving balance. It tends to be a continuous process of gain-

FIGURE 2-1

ing, deliberately losing, and then regaining one's balance, all in a well-controlled moving state. Both of these abilities are vital to good play.

We can also get moving by deliberately breaking the rules governing stability. Since moving (instability) is the opposite of stability (balance) you can get moving simply by putting your center of gravity outside (beyond) your base of support in any direction you desire to move and you will automatically be on the move. For instance, a start in sprint racing takes advantage of a loss of balance (Figure 2-2). A high center of gravity and a reduced (or small) base of support could also contribute to initiating this movement (Figure 2-3).

FIGURE 2-2

FIGURE 2-3

When losing balance you will tend to start moving some-what rapidly and without effort, since the pull of gravity will help do the job for you. Can you see why some have described running as a series of falls in which runners continually lose and catch their balance (Figure 2-4)? Can you find situations in which losing balance contributes to a quick start? Can you see how and why one must shift one's center of gravity to maintain balance when stopping or changing directions?

An uncontrolled loss of balance could lead to a serious in-jury in some circumstances and may have to be avoided by incorporating one or more of the principles of balance. Can you find specific situations in which you could help another or

FIGURE 2-4

yourself avoid a loss of balance by employing one or more of the three balance principles?

HOW TO IMPROVE YOUR BALANCE

• Understand and apply the mechanical principles of balance. Consider these in varied and real situations.

• Explore and practice a variety of static and dynamic balance positions. Remember that games and other movement activities can be an excellent source of balance practice if carefully selected. Also remember that one can learn at any age to adapt more effectively to messages received from visual input, the semicircular canals in the ears, pressures on the body, and the proprioceptors (a sensory system found within the muscles and tendons).

• Because being able to relax improves your reception and

responses to the messages sent by body mechanisms it is vital that those who need to improve their balance learn to relax and that the environment in which they move be initially as emotionally supportive as possible until they can remain relaxed under progressively more stressful conditions.

• Develop sufficient muscular strength and endurance to be able to make necessary balance adjustments.

If you wish to improve balance while standing, landing, moving, or stopping suddenly, encourage the following:

1. Bend the knees instead of keeping them straight. (Can you see the important role the knees play in both lowering the center of gravity and allowing the body weight to be adjusted over the base of support?)
2. Spread the feet to increase the base of support; don't keep them close together.
3. When stopping suddenly lean away from, not toward, the direction you were moving to keep the center of gravity over the base of support.
4. When landing or stopping suddenly keep your head up and look forward. Don't look at the ground by dropping your head forward. (Can you see how dropping your head forward would shift your weight forward, possibly decreasing your stability?)

Two additional comments need to be made about the base of support and good balance. First, if you are going to receive a force that could push your center of gravity beyond your base of support you may need to shift your weight toward the oncoming force and widen your base of support in that direction to maintain your balance. Adapting to a stride position with a lean into the oncoming force may not only allow you to absorb the force gradually in a rocking motion but it may also be useful as a preparatory movement for your next action.

Second, a long, narrow base of support can make balance in the narrow direction difficult because it reduces your adaptive potential in that direction. Spread your feet out considerably wider than your shoulders. Now have seomeone push you gently from behind. Can you feel the effect of too wide a base? Now place your feet directly below your shoulders and ask someone to push again. Compare the two.

OBSERVATIONS AND ACTIVITIES

Observe sports events. When players must change direction suddenly what do they do to maintain their moving (dynamic) balance? Note the lean. How does this affect their center of gravity? What about the size of their base of support? How do they position their feet? How much of their foot is in contact with the ground? You will understand the function of this practice and its relationship to maintaining balance after you have read chapter 4 on absorbing force. Can friction on a rough surface affect balance by helping a player absorb force? Can a lack of friction on a smooth surface make it more difficult to maintain balance? How do the different kinds of footwear worn in different sports, on different surfaces, and under varying conditions help in maintaining balance?

Note how the degree of stability is determined by how directly the weight is centered over the base of support. Can you see the adaptive function the knees and other joints play in this situation? Note how the skilled performers shift their center of gravity toward an oncoming force to allow for good balance adjustment as the center of gravity is pushed backward. This is similar to leaning into the wind when you are walking on a very windy day.

Do various playing positions and situations require varying degrees of stability and instability? Can you see examples of this in football? If a player was uncertain as to what would happen next, what position (in relation to the center of gravity and the base of support) might prove most effective? Can you relate this to boxing, fencing, tag? Does good balance seem to have any effect on a player's ability to make rapid adjustments?

What does a football blocker do to unbalance the opponent? Does a blocker lift the opponent's center of gravity? Attempt to push the opponent's center of gravity beyond the base of support? Attempt to reduce the opponent's base of support? Can you see why pushing without lifting would not be as effective?

Might a wrestler push and lift in a similar way? Can you see why poor posture might decrease good balance? How does the pole used in tightrope walking aid the performer's balance? Consider the adaptability factor in relation to shifting the center of gravity for lateral (side to side) balance. Can you see how the nonracket arm in tennis is important in maintaining good balance? Who might have more stability, a tall or short player? A player with even weight distribution or a player with a large upper trunk?

Can you see where a lack of flexibility could affect balance adjustment potential in some instances? Can you determine situations in which a senior citizen's balance could be affected by a lack of flexibility? Looking at Figure 5-6 can you see how an athlete whose iliopsoas muscles are "tight" could be pulled into a swayback position? Could this have an effect on balance? Note both the position of the center of gravity and the adaptability factor.

Can you see how tension or tension-producing stress could affect balance? Can you see why running is faster than jogging? Where is the center of gravity in relation to the base of support (Figure 2-5)? Can you see how the direction of lean could initiate the forward or backward movement in tumbling and gymnastics (Figure 2-6)?

Some individuals may have a sense of queasiness or awkwardness when putting their bodies into new positions or positions not experienced for some time. This is a normal response and will diminish as involvement continues. Encouraging relaxation helps.

• Practice moving in slow motion. Challenge yourself with difficult balance positions.

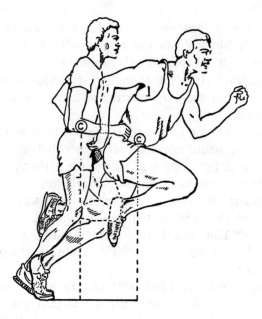

FIGURE 2-5

FIGURE 2-6

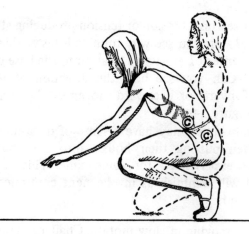

• Our eyes are important in helping us to balance. Try to balance on one foot. Now close your eyes. If you are going to stay balanced you must learn to use other sources of information.

• Indian wrestle. With hands gripped as shown in Figure 2-7, a good base of support, and knees bent to lower the center of gravity, each participant attempts to force the other off balance. You might be able to equalize two people of different abilities by having the winner of each trial go on to a more difficult balance position to challenge him- or herself on the next trial (for example, a long, narrow base of support with one foot directly in line with the other or knees straight and stiff).

FIGURE 2-7

• Do a basketball defense shuffle or shadow practice. Take a guarding position. Attempt to shadow (follow exactly) a moving player. Note how you use your feet, ankles, knees, and other body parts to help you change directions and maintain balance.

FIGURE 2-8

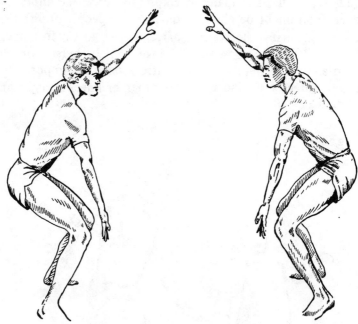

• Run and come to a sudden stop. How do you maintain your balance? Observe someone who tends to lose balance when stopping. Can you determine which mechanical principles she or he needs to work on?

• Try the following games for improving balance.

Frantic Ball. Have each player place a ball on the floor and roll it, using only the feet. The objective is to keep all balls moving at all times and to see how long the round can be extended. If a ball stops or goes out of a predetermined area a point is lost, and the round ends when a total of five points have been lost. You will need one ball for each player, plus a few extra balls so that players will have to be responsible for more than just their original ball. This mixing tends to increase the amount of balancing involved. Constantly adjusting balance is what contributes to growth and development in this area. Old, worn out tennis balls are excellent for this game. To avoid the possibility of a kicking injury you may want participants to play barefoot. If the balls are being lifted off the floor, which can be dangerous, you can also deduct a point for lifting. The official might like to use a whistle to indicate each loss of a point and use a stopwatch to help measure improvement or establish a record. If you play in an enclosed space, players can be allowed to play balls off the wall. If you need to play in an open space, you may want to use natural boundaries, such as the edge of an asphalt area, or you can have some players serve as sidelines players who can send the ball into the playing area. Although it is best to play on a flat surface, you can play on a grassy area, but you will need to reduce the number of balls used.

Carpet Activities. Each participant stands on a piece of carpet and moves by "twisting" or rotating his or her hips (no "scooting" allowed). This type of movement not only develops balance but also builds the abdominal muscles, which are extremely helpful in keeping the center of gravity over the base of support. If players have great difficulty maintaining their balance while twisting have them use a smaller piece of carpet under each foot and use a cross country skiing type of movement. All kinds of tag and snatch games, relays, hockey-like games, and other variations can be played.

These games and many others that develop balance skills can be found in *Follow Me.*

• Observe a person who appears clumsy. Can you determine if any of the principles of balance are being violated? What suggestions might you make?

chapter three

Initiating movement

Do you need to be fast, forceful, or both? The answer to this question will help you determine what you might do to get started.

Every time we begin to move or change directions we must first deal with *inertia*. Inertia is sometimes thought of as a state of stillness, but this definition is incomplete since inertia can be a still or moving state. Inertia is actually any present state of being and overcoming inertia involves a change in that state and the resistance to that change. It could be a change in either speed (faster or slower) or direction. Change of any kind requires a force to overcome inertia (our present state). In this chapter we will deal only with ways to help overcome inertia to initiate a move.

Many people do not give a great deal of consideration to this initial aspect of moving, but it is a vital component and may very well determine whether success or failure will follow. It can affect the amount of force that can be generated and how quickly we can accomplish a given task. Tasks usually require force, speed, or varying combinations of these components. So we must clearly delineate what we are attempting to do, determine whether force or speed is most important to the specific task, and, understanding that various options are available to us and that some of these options can more effectively meet our needs than others, select the way we will initiate our move based upon the given task at hand. Decisions are task or goal specific and it is important to know where you are going and how soon you must be there before you choose how to get started.

GETTING READY TO MOVE

• Are you physiologically ready? Are you warmed up for the task? Warming the body increases the blood flow and reduces the sluggishness of body tissues and fluids.

FIGURE 3-1

We can compare the fluidlike state within the body tissues to the oil in your car. If you start your car when it is cold the oil is thicker. Once the car is running the oil warms and becomes thinner. Now the engine can work less to accomplish the same task, since the counteracting forces have been reduced, increasing the freedom of movement. As you play be sure you warm up and remain warm. This will allow you to move more quickly and forcefully and avoid injuries that could occur if you were not sufficiently internally warmed.

• Are you anatomically ready? You save time if you already have your involved joints bent or unlocked and the muscles to be used on a partial stretch. Bending the joints in preparation for the move can put the muscles to be used on a partial stretch.

Watch anyone begin to move. They must initiate the movement by bending the involved joints. Find a tennis, softball, or volleyball player who stands upright with knees straight and you can assume that this person will start to move more slowly than necessary. A muscle that is stretched has a greater number of muscle fibers ready for involvement. A muscle fiber that is already shortened cannot contract to cause movement to occur. To keep the knees slightly bent does require more effort, but well-toned muscles can maintain this position without fatigue. In fact, this very act will help to maintain the needed muscle tone and keep the muscles warm.

Two of my Little League coach-friends, Bob Gallagher and Ed Dunn, use a clever technique to accomplish this position of readiness. They tell their players to be like gorillas. It works! Not only is the word "gorilla" a quick, positive reminder, but it and the technique that goes with it can be easily remembered.

The bent-knee ready position is also important because by bending the knees one automatically lowers the center of gravity for better balance. This position also allows for a shift of weight (center of gravity in relation to the base of support) to adjust more rapidly to the unexpected. Wrestlers, fencers, or tag players who rarely get tagged must be ready at all times for whatever happens. Observe their body position.

The value of stretching a muscle before using it will be discussed further in Chapter 4.

Perhaps bent knees are the key to increased success in many activities.

• A full and rapid backswing can stimulate the stretch reflex, which assists in rapidly overcoming inertia during initial acceleration.

Sensory receptors, called muscles spindles, are stimulated when skeletal muscles are forcefully stretched. These receptors are part of a reflex mechanism that "fires" a message to the spinal cord. Since reflex impulses travel only to the spinal cord and not on to the higher nervous system the responding impulse for the muscle to contract is very rapid. Thus, while the stretch reflex mechanism protects the muscles against being overstretched and torn it can also help us to overcome inertia very rapidly in the initial period of acceleration. This becomes important in force development since momentum is the product of mass times velocity. It is also important that a player does not confuse the use of the stretch reflex to overcome inertia (thus allowing more force to be developed over the available distance) with the rapid completion of an action. One needs to be aware that to evoke the stretch reflex requires *additional* time during the preparation phase.

A muscle that is not well conditioned could be damaged if it is rapidly or forcibly stretched. For this reason you should maintain adequate muscle development and be warmed up before deliberately involving the stretch reflex.

Watch the preparatory phase of a pitcher, a field goal kicker, a weight lifter. Can you see how they use the stretch reflex to their advantage? Golfers and tennis players also use it to gain greater force when they wish to send the ball a long distance.

FIGURE 3-2

• In some situations you can use the pull of gravity to initiate movement quickly.

As we noted in Chapter 2 by creating a situation in which the center of gravity is beyond the base of support a condition of instability or movement occurs. Sprinters, football line players, and gymnasts frequently use this source of force to help them move (Figure 3-3).

Have you ever observed a child who rocks backward before getting started in the direction he or she wishes to go? This rocking action will increase the force that can be applied to the

FIGURE 3-3

rear foot but it may take time, causing the child a slow start. In activities in which the player must initiate movement rapidly to be successful this child may be tagged, slow to reach base, or hit by the oncoming dodge ball. There are times when it is more important to sacrifice a specific force technique for one that allows for a more rapid completion of the task by getting started rapidly. If this child could learn to use gravity to initiate his or her movements rapidly rather than using a rear-foot push, success in these activities might be enhanced.

As you move try to find ways to use the pull of gravity to your advantage in overcoming inertia. Can you find at least one way you can use gravity to help you move more effectively?

• Shorten levers to get there faster with less force.

There are times when force may become secondary, less important, or even unnecessary. Starting rapidly, completing a task in a given amount of time, being ready for the next move, repeating a motion several times as rapidly as possible, or even reducing or absorbing force that may interfere with the successful completion of a task may become the primary objective.

If a quick move or change is needed and force is not a primary factor, shortening the involved levers may help. (See the section in chapter 4 on lever length.) Arms, legs, and the trunk are actually all levers. Note the difference between a short-distance runner and a marathoner. Observe how much more rapidly the sprinter's legs come around. This requires more energy expenditure, but it allows for increased speed when that is your primary concern. To accomplish this the legs (levers) are shortened by bending the knees more. The arms are flexed to allow the rotation time of the arms and legs to be synchronized.

A short throw from the infield to first base, a "flick" in badminton, a block volley at the net in tennis, a bunt in softball or baseball, all require little force but need a rapid response for success. This can be accomplished by shortening the lever (in these instances the arms), by bending the joints, and by reducing any unnecessary backswing. As a spectator observe the techniques used in these skills. Find other uses of the short lever, for example, notice figure skaters' arms when they wish to increase the speed of their spin (rotation).

Inexperienced players sometimes have difficulty with reducing the force factor. I carry with me one enlarged knuckle on my right hand from such a basketball teammate, who literally moved the top two segments of my finger into a new relationship with the rest of my hand (Figure 3-4).

Excitement and a sense of all-out effort characterize the inexperienced player, who may have to be helped to realize that "forcefully" and "quickly" sometimes need to be separated and that skill is involved in knowing when and how to execute each successfully.

ACTIVITIES

• *Warm up to reduce internal resistance.* Place your hand in cold water for a minute. Then remove it and try to move your fingers rapidly. Is it difficult at first? Does it become easier after awhile? Why?

FIGURE 3-4

• *Joints in ready position with muscles on a partial stretch.* Standing tall with knees straight, have someone shout a directional command while you attempt to move as rapidly as possible in that direction. What is the first thing that happens to your knees to make this movement possible? Now repeat, but start in a ready position. Do you feel the difference in how quickly you can initiate your response?

• *Involvement of the stretch reflex.* Avoiding a deep knee bend, first jump and reach as high as you can using a half-squat involving a dip or bounce to induce the stretch reflex. Record your best height. Then, after you have rested, jump and reach again using a half-squat but no dip or bounce. Record the best height you can reach. Then compare the two.

• *Use of gravity to overcome inertia.* Attempt some movements that you initiate with a loss of balance. Is inertia overcome rapidly? Can you learn to control this loss of balance so as much of the fall as possible is used to your benefit?

• *Shorten lever when maximum force is not needed.* Place a ball on the ground. Ask a player to stand about ten feet away. Moving to the ball, pick it up, and, without a backswing, throw it to this player. It might be wise to ask this player to wear a glove.

• *Shorten lever to reduce preparation time.* If you are a tennis player or would like a real challenge, try playing the block volley at the net without a backswing and with the ball closer to you so you can use a short lever. Be sure you know the proper technique for executing the block volley before you begin.

chapter four

Force

After you initiate an action you will usually need to continue to develop sufficient force to accomplish the task effectively. The amount of force you will need is directly related to your task objective. Your goal should be to skillfully develop and apply only the necessary amount of force in the most effective way. Involving too much or too little force or applying it inappropriately may actually interfere with meeting your objective. This chapter will discuss how to develop and apply force to affect movement. But you will need to relate this information to your specific needs in a given situation and make appropriate applications.

FORCE DEVELOPMENT

- Each contributing body part can add to the amount of force developed *(summation)*.

FIGURE 4-1

If maximum force is needed then all contributing parts must be involved to their maximum extent.

To ensure maximum participation of all contributing body parts you need to use the following:

1. opposition (involving opposite sides of the upper and lower body)
2. fully stretching the involved muscles before using them, by actions such as full backswing and full trunk rotation
3. weight transfer
4. follow-through
5. sufficient strength of each contributing body part
6. full range of motion of all involved joints (available and used)
7. maximal effort by each contributing body part.

When less than maximum force is needed some factors can be appropriately modified:

1. Involved muscles are not put on a full stretch—backswing may be reduced, trunk rotation may be reduced.
2. Each body part makes less than maximal contribution.

All other factors are usually maintained for the contributions they make to other aspects of movement, such as balance and accuracy.

If rapid completion of a task is vital to the success of the movement and little force is required it appears most appropriate for:

1. opposition to be considered fairly irrelevant
2. the backswing to be reduced or eliminated
3. the range of motion of the involved joints to be reduced (levers shortened).

Other factors are usually maintained for the contributions they make to other aspects of movement.

• Each contributing body segment picks up the flow of motion in sequence as the preceding body part has reached its peak contribution. This produces a continual increase in force development *(sequential involvement),* illustrated in Figure 4-2.

Force development normally originates from the center of gravity of the body and flows outward toward the end of the involved extremity.

To ensure appropriate sequential build up of force these factors need to be present:

1. All body parts in the sequence must be in appropriate condition to participate. Any weak area can interfere with the sequential force buildup and substantially diminish the force that has already been developed.

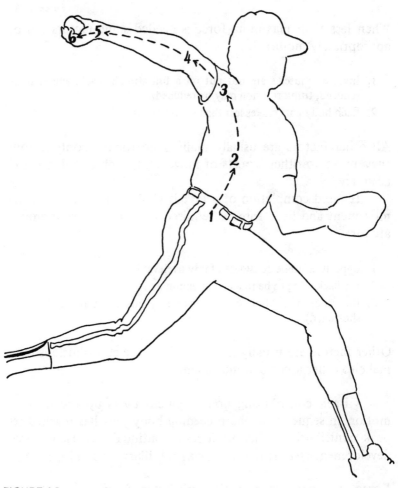

FIGURE 4-2

2. A player must be able to "set" (stabilize) previously involved parts of the body so that those coming later in the sequence have a firm foundation to pull against to make their contribution.

Two exceptions occur in the "pacing" of force development and involve the need for less than maximal force:

1. The "push" type of move that might be involved in a golf putt; a low, short serve in badminton; or a punch volley at the net in tennis is usually executed by a steady, controlled timing with the outer parts of the extremity not joining in the sequence so force is not "building."

2. Moves that may require an absorption of force at or near the conclusion of the act, such as the bunt, feint, or drop shot, require a reversal of the normal buildup of force.

• For force to develop, some portion of the body must be stabilized. This stabilized part acts as a brace against which the moving part(s) can push or pull and also prevents the absorption of force that would occur if there were no stabilization.

Many less experienced participants have neglected the role that the stabilizers play in force production. Many weekend golfers, for instance, are not aware of the role the abdominal muscles play in the distance of their drives (Figure 4-3).

The abdominals stabilize the hips and create the anchor point around which the swing and weight transfer take place. The abdominals play a similar role in soccer, and the shoulder girdle has a stabilizing role in throwing or in striking.

Children and individuals who seem unable to jump, throw, kick, or hit with any degree of success or vigor are frequently lacking in the area of stabilization. Before they can benefit from learning a technique for a specific skill they must attain adequate development of the muscles involved and of the stabilizers. This will be discussed further in chapter 5 on preparing the body to apply the mechanical principles of movement.

• Proper weight transfer can contribute substantially to force buildup.

To prepare for weight transfer your weight may be initially shifted in the direction opposite that of the action phase. This

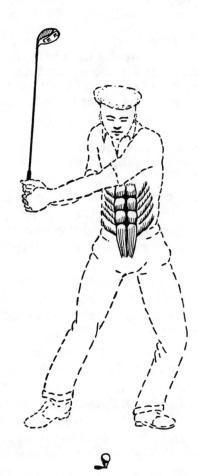

FIGURE 4-3

preparatory transfer allows for a more total weight transfer and can pull some of the muscles that will be used during the action phase into a more effective elongated or stretched position for greater force development. This may also stimulate appropriate stretch reflexes, thus assisting you to overcome inertia rapidly. The shift of weight in the direction you wish to apply force during the action phase increases the velocity at which the whole body is moving.

This weight transfer also assists in timing and accuracy since transferring the body weight from the back foot to the

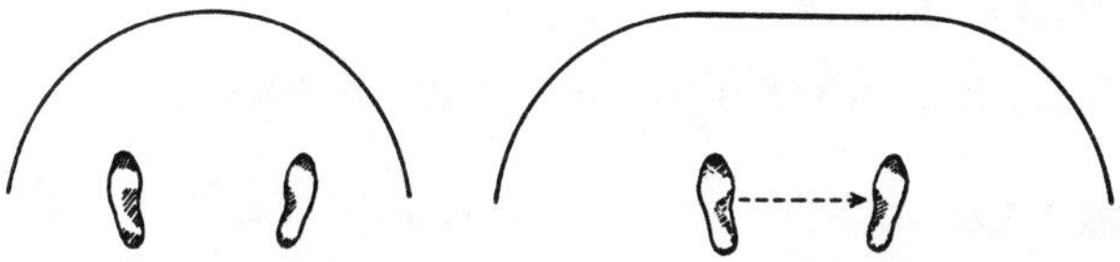

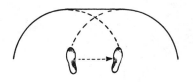

FIGURE 4-4

forward foot allows for a flattening of the swinging arc, permitting you to release the throw or stroke or strike the object at several points in your forward movement without sacrificing accuracy (see chapter 8).

When there is no weight transfer the swinging arc tends to be a perfect circle; a weight transfer allows for the swinging arc to be flattened. This occurs because your swinging arc takes the center of gravity as its center and as you shift weight your center of gravity also shifts. So you start making one arc from your initial center of gravity position and end swinging around a second center of gravity position. These two arcs overlap creating a single longer arc with a flattened area caused by the shift of weight and center of gravity.

FIGURE 4-5

This is extremely helpful to the beginner whose timing may be less than perfect, and it allows the highly skilled player to strike or release later in the flattened arc pattern, increasing the time and distance over which force can be developed before contact or release. The final weight transfer continues over a bent forward knee into the follow-through. This allows for the gradual absorption of force. Follow through over a bent knee also aids in keeping the center of gravity low and over the base of support, thus avoiding a loss of balance that could negatively affect consistency, accuracy, and preparation for the next move.

• Force buildup requires time and distance.

By putting the muscles to be involved on a full stretch before use (as in a preparatory backswing, crouch, or trunk bend or rotation) the time and distance over which force is developed can be increased.

Summation, opposition, weight transfer, lengthening the lever, and flattening the swinging arc can also increase the time and distance over which force develops. The elimination of any of the above, which might occur if the act needed to be rushed, could substantially reduce force development.

Some participants reduce the time and distance over which force is developed believing that rushing contributes to maximum force development. The confusion lies between getting the action done the most quickly or the most forcefully. This misconception normally fades with experience.

FIGURE 4-6

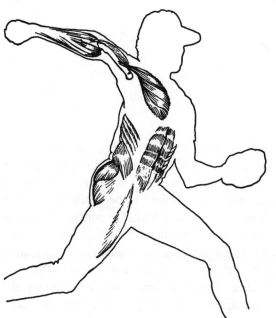

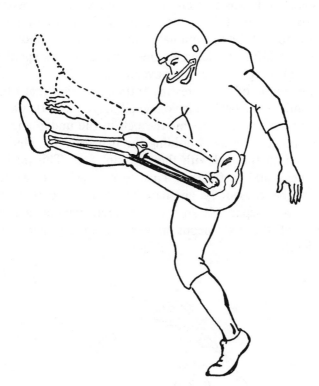

FIGURE 4-7

Good range of motion (ROM) can also be an important factor in increasing the time and distance over which one can develop force. If, for example, the ROM in your shoulder joint is limited by tight chest muscles or joint restrictions you may be limited in your backswing or reach (Figure 4-6).

Tight quadriceps (found on the front of your upper leg) could reduce the preparatory backswing of your leg, while tight hamstrings (found on the back of your upper leg) could limit how far you could follow through on the kick (Figure 4-7).

• Extraneous movements may reduce or inhibit force production.

Any movement that does not contribute directly to the movement objective is wasteful and may even require compensating efforts to counteract its effect. One of the goals of practice should be to reduce or eliminate any unnecessary movement. Observe a skillful participant, then watch an inexperienced player. Can you spot the extra movements?

An example of an interesting extra movement that I found among some of my beginning volleyball players was that as they moved the striking arm to hit the ball in the underhand serve they also moved the hand holding the ball forward. Thus they literally chased the ball with their striking arm. This made the contact weak and ineffective. This "overflow" or extra movement may be caused by an inability to use the body parts selectively and separately in a coordinated manner; a lack of awareness of this extraneous movement; or a general overall tension level.

FIGURE 4-8

• Noncontributing tension retards the buildup of force and is counterproductive.

Reciprocal innervation is a process by which dual messages stimulate specific muscles to contract while the opposing muscle groups receive a message to relax. This allows the contraction to occur without countering resistances.

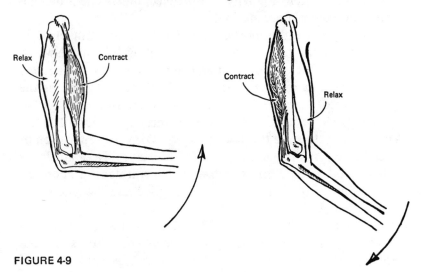

FIGURE 4-9

Often the beginner or one who has great desire to succeed develops a residual, nonproductive tension in the muscles that need to be relaxed. This excess tension inhibits the freedom and flow of movement.

During stressful situations you can observe even the highly skilled attempting to reduce their tension level. Note the swimmer or runner who shakes out before going to the blocks, the golfer who takes a practice swing before the crucial putt, the basketball player who stretches before a foul shot.

Being aware of the effect of tension can help. You can also learn to relax more. This skill can benefit many aspects of living and should be aided by participation in play experiences.

FORCE APPLICATION

- Force must be applied in the desired direction.

To be effective, force must be applied in the desired direction. In striking a ball, for example, the force is applied directly through the center of gravity of the object unless one is deliberately seeking a spin or rotation.

A very old and important principle of motion involved in directional application of force is Newton's well-known law: To every action there is an equal and opposite reaction. One way to interpret this statement is to think of the "action" as the application of force and the "equal and opposite reaction" as the resistance or resistive response to this application of force. Another way to state this law might be: To every application of force there is an equal and opposite resistance. Now all this is followed by a result or response, which will depend upon the relationship of the amount of force applied and the amount of resistance met.

Two possibilities are: (1) The object of resistance is movable and the force is sufficient to move it. The result is that the resisting object moves in the direction of the application of force. Examples might be hitting a ball, pushing a car, throwing, or kicking. (2) The object of resistance is immovable (the earth or a wall) and so the force applied cannot move it. The result is that the source of force moves in the direction opposite to the application of force. Examples might be jumping, running, walking, or hitting a ball against a wall. If the resisting object and the source of force are both movable they will both respond to the force and move away from each other. Examples occur in billiards or with a bowling ball and pins.

Thus if you want to move *forward* you need to push *backward* in swimming or running. If you want to jump *upward* you must push *down*.

Can you see how starting blocks help direct the force in a more desirable direction?

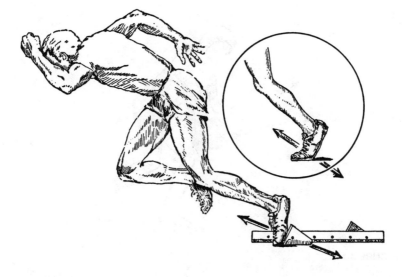

FIGURE 4-10

Perhaps less obvious is the fact that if you want an object to go *up* you must hit *under* it (volleyball set); if you want it to go *straight ahead* you must hit *behind* it (line drive); if you want it to go *down* you must hit on *top* of it (tennis serve, volleyball spike). We can also use this information to analyze errors. An object that was not hit upward enough was not hit underneath enough, and one that was hit upward too much was hit too far underneath. To correct these errors emphasis must be put on the appropriate contact points. (See the section on contact point in Chapter 8 and Figure 4-11.)

Application of force in any direction other than the desired one can lead to an undesirable result. A tennis stroke can be very forceful, but if the ball is hit upward or too far to the side this force can lead to failure (out of bounds play). In swimming, where the force is applied throughout the action phase, force application that counters the desired direction of propulsion is not only wasteful but may require additional compensatory effort or lead to weaving or bobbing.

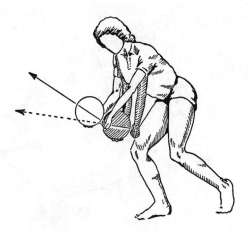

FIGURE 4-11

• When the goal is maximum distance the angle of release, impact, or takeoff may determine the effective application of the developed force.

Because many projectiles have a predetermined parabolic path, it has been possible to study the effect of various angles of release, takeoff, and impact. A forty-five-degree angle will normally gain maximum distance when the initial and touch-down points are on the same level, as in a golf stroke or place kick. If the projectile or center of gravity of a human projectile travels from a point higher than it will land, as in a home

FIGURE 4-12

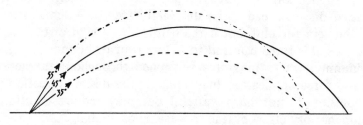

run, punt, shot put, broad jump, or javelin throw, the angle should be reduced slightly to compensate. Of course if you had to golf from a lower level to a higher elevation the reverse would hold true. If there were wind conditions or the object were affected by other air flows this principle would have to be modified according to these variables.

• A good follow-through insures maximum velocity and force at the point of release or impact.

An important and perceptive question that is sometimes raised is how can the follow-through, which follows the application of force, have an effect on force application? A complete and extended follow-through assures that the slowing down process will not be initiated too early during the final part of the action phase. This means that maximum velocity is still available at impact, release, or other time of need. The effects of the very subtle error of slowing down are perhaps more obvious if you observe inexperienced runners who, seeing the finish line, slow down as they approach it.

A complete follow-through also allows for a gradual absorption of force, preventing injuries like muscle tears or loss of balance. Thus a good follow-through plays several important roles in the effective application of force.

ABSORBING FORCE

Although there are times when we need to develop force there are also times when to avoid injury, stop a movement, or maintain balance or control, a force needs to be absorbed. When these situations occur knowing how to absorb a force is of real value and may mean the difference between success and failure or injury.

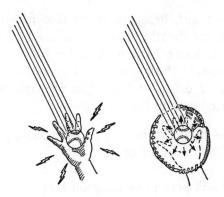

FIGURE 4-13

Force can be reduced by *giving with* and/or *spreading* the force. *Giving* with the force slows it down gradually over time and distance. Our joints allow us to accomplish this by bending (giving gradually) as we receive the force.

FIGURE 4-14

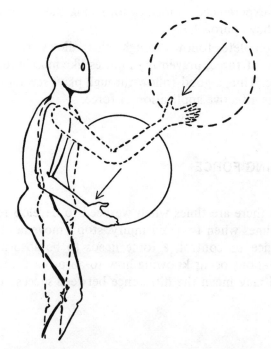

Spreading the force out over a larger receiving area means that no single part of the area takes as much of the total force. The larger the area receiving the force the less the impact force on any part of that area.

Note carefully the difference in the size of the impact area in figures 4-15 and 4-16. Which would tend to be less injurious? Although the hard part of the shoulder pads in football does not "give" it does spread the received force out over the entire surface of the hard part of the pad thus reducing the concentration of the impact.

Can you see how a catcher's mitt both gives and spreads the force of impact? Can you see that in landing you would need to give with your ankles, knees, hips, and vertebral column by allowing them to bend to control and absorb the force of your weight? If you fell while landing might you want to have the fleshier parts (which are also larger) of your body take the impact both to give and to spread the force?

Can you see why a ball that is somewhat deflated would hurt less in a game such as dodge ball? Can you also see why the ball would be less apt to roll or bounce away? Or how a good pair of tennis shoes could help give and spread force in stop-

FIGURE 4-15

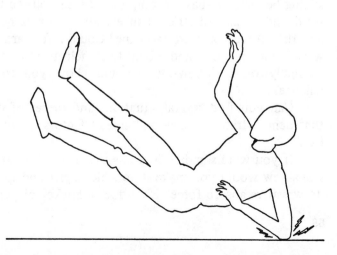

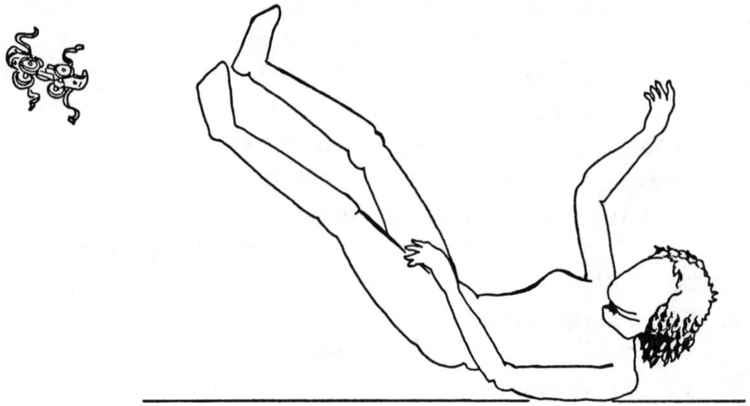

FIGURE 4-16

ping? Or how a judo or karate participant rolls to spread the impact of landing over a large body area?

Can you see why a quick stop is made more effective by putting your whole foot down and letting the knees bend? How does leaning backward allow you more time and distance over which to absorb force? Can you see how friction could help spread the force? When sliding into base one wants to first avoid being tagged, but how is the need to absorb force to prevent sliding beyond the base accomplished? Can you see how a forward and backward stride stance could at times help you to absorb a force you were receiving? Could a forward and backward stance position and a bent knee help to reduce the force gradually on a follow-through and allow you to maintain balance?

Can you find several situations and pieces of equipment that demonstrate the give and spread factors in force absorption?

If you were standing in a bus that made several starts and stops how would you make it possible to give and spread? How do wrestlers absorb force? How does a hockey player control a fast-moving pass? How does a ball player control the force of a pitch when bunting?

Can you find a variety of situations in which force absorption allows for further control or the avoidance of injury? Can you see how good range of motion (ROM) could help in the absorption of force over time and distance and possibly prevent small tears within the muscles? Would the strength required to slow force down gradually have an important role?

Can you see why runners and joggers are discouraged from running on very hard surfaces with little give? Do basketball floors give at all?

OPPOSITION

Opposition, the involvement of the opposite sides of the upper and lower body, plays several roles in relation to force. Opposition makes it possible to have:

1. a longer preparatory backswing as well as a more complete follow-through, which increases the time and distance over which force can be generated and applied
2. more total muscle involvement through summation and sequence
3. a full stretch of the trunk muscles before their contraction
4. greater transfer of weight, allowing the body weight to participate fully in force development
5. a better balanced position throughout the movement, creating a more stable base from which the mover can push to increase force
6. greater ease in adjusting the center of gravity over the base of support for good balance
7. a position that can absorb a received force and also be prepared for the next move.

Failing to use opposition is a common error among the very young, the inexperienced, or those who have developed their own "style." It is so common among the young and inexperi-

Lacking opposition   Moving in opposition

FIGURE 4-17

enced that it is considered part of the growth and development process. If opposition has not occurred naturally through experience it should be encouraged. At first the change may feel awkward, but an individual can adjust with patience and perseverance. After players have begun to feel comfortable with this new position have them attempt several throws for distance from each position. Can they observe any measurable difference?

There are some exceptions to the use of opposition in specific sports or for specific reasons. Some badminton players have preferred not to use opposition in the low, short serve to protect more easily against a quick backhand return. Fencers do not use opposition because they prefer to make minimal contact surface available to their opponent.

LEVER LENGTH

The longer the lever the greater the force potential at the end of it. Lengthening the lever, of course, may be of no value if the length prohibits physical control of the lever, reduces the participant's ability to move it through a complete pattern, or reduces the ability to complete the act in the time available.

Length of lever affects both rotary speed and force. A shortened lever can be brought around or rotated more rapidly but will normally have relatively less force; the lengthened lever may be harder and slower to rotate, but it will be able to build up considerably more velocity over the additional distance. Thus a full reach (not crowding the ball or not choking up on the striking instrument) may help one hit a home run or have a more forceful tennis stroke, but it will require a longer time to execute. This creates no time problem in movements such as the tennis serve or a golf drive, but a fast pitch might get by you during the time required to take the "long" swing. When this occurs you may choose a shorter lever with less force so you can get around in time to meet the ball. If the oncoming object is traveling this fast you may be able to utilize the momentum of the ball to contribute to your force rather than developing force through the use of a long lever.

If your objective is to react quickly or increase the speed of rotation such as in a net play in tennis, a concealed bunt, sprinting, a multiple somersault dive, a skater's spin, a short throw, or a quick kick it would be more effective if you use a shorter lever. But if your objective is force and you have sufficient time, distance, and strength to accomplish the specific task you could be more successful if you applied a longer lever, such as in a baseline tennis stroke, a home run, a marathon, a swan dive, "ring-a-bell" at a carnival, a long throw, or a long kick.

In relation to the above information can you answer the following questions? If you wanted to do as many somersaults as possible in a dive, how could you most effectively accomplish this? If you wanted to make a dive appear slow and graceful in air, how could this be accomplished? Can you see any application of this to gymnastics?

What would happen if skaters drew their arms in to their bodies when they were spinning? Does this have anything to do with a pivot in basketball?

Tennis net play requires rapid reactions but less stroke force. How would your net stroke differ from your baseline strokes? Note that since the force needs are reduced the length of the backswing can also be reduced.

In making the choice of whether to use a longer or shorter lever it is also important to realize that a quick movement may consume proportionately more energy for the amount of movement accomplished since it does not take full advantage of momentum and the increased time and distance available to develop force. If people attempted to sprint a marathon, they would probably find themselves exhausted early in the race. Each situation requires the participant's consideration of the factors involved—this is part of the fun of participation.

OBSERVATIONS AND ACTIVITIES

It is helpful to observe unskilled individuals. Can you see any common faults in their force development?

When trying for maximum force do they use opposition? Do they really put the muscles to be used on a full stretch? Do they shorten their backswing and rush the preparatory phase? Do they use any unnecessary movements? Does their motion flow, or do they hesitate at any time during a movement, thus breaking the sequential timing of the involved body parts? Can you see a real and complete weight transfer? Do they use a complete follow-through? Can they adapt to varying task needs (objectives)? Can they develop only the amount of force that is needed? Can they reduce the time needed to complete a time-limited task such as a short throw or a bunt? Can they reduce or eliminate the backswing if it is not needed? Can they effectively shorten as well as lengthen a lever for an appropriate result? Are they tense? Can they "set" (stabilize) various parts of their body to help them move well? Do they apply force in the desired direction?

Observe several joggers. Try to find one who toes out severely when running. Can you see the body rotation from the force being pushed out to the side rather than backward? Can you relate this to Newton's law of action and reaction? Try to find one who has a great deal of up and down motion. Can you see that this person is pushing downward more than backward? If these joggers are out for the exercise they are meeting their objective, but if they wish to use their efforts most efficiently, do their best, or avoid stress on body parts they may need to change their style.

If you are able to observe a shot-putter or a golfer going for distance, attempt to calculate the angle of object projection. Remember, straight up is ninety degrees and an angle one-half this would be forty-five degrees.

- *Summation:* Play catch. In attempting to throw for distance utilize various amounts of backswing. Compare your results.
- *Length of Lever:* Find a piece of Styrofoam large enough to allow nails to enter it to approximately two or three inches, about eighteen inches long and at least a couple inches wide. Attach a weight to a piece of string roughly sixteen inches long. Attach this to the top of your piece of Styrofoam. Place two nails into the face of the Styrofoam, one approximately fifteen inches from the top and one roughly eight inches from the top.

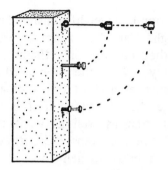

FIGURE 4-18

Now, holding the string parallel to the ground, let it swing free and hit the nail at fifteen inches. (Note: If you are having difficulty with the weight missing the nail place the whole device next to a wall and let the string swing along the wall.) Shorten the string to eight inches and let the weight swing. Is the nail hit by the weight at fifteen inches driven deeper than the nail hit by the weight at eight inches? What does this tell us about the force developed at the end of a longer and shorter lever?

Put an eyelet screw or nail into a wall. Pass the end of the string through the eyelet or over the nail. Now start the weight swinging free. As it swings pull up on the string (shortening it) and then let it again swing long. What happens to the speed at which the string is swinging? Does this say anything about the speed of rotation of a long and short lever? Can you think of several different situations in which each might apply?

• *Weight Transfer:* Set up a batting tee or a traffic cone. If you do not have these an inexpensive batting tee can be constructed from old rubber tubing, an empty plastic bottle, a cardboard box and your imagination. Hang a sturdy backdrop on the clothes line so you can hit into it. Bat the ball several times using a complete weight transfer each time. Listen to the impact, feel the force. Now, trying to keep your weight centered between your feet (no weight transfer), take several more hits. Is there a different feeling of force? Does the impact sound different? If you had more difficulty hitting the ball or hitting it straight ahead when you did not transfer your weight can you relate this problem to the pattern of the swinging arc in the two different styles? In which style does the swinging arc tend to flatten more? Why?

• *Opposition:* Play catch using opposition and not using opposition. Compare the distance of your throws.

• *Angle of Projection:* Try this experiment outdoors when there is no wind. Take a garden hose. Turn on the water. Holding the nozzle at ground level, aim the stream of water at various angles. At which angle does the water go the farthest? If you can't tell set up some cans as targets. Hold the nozzle about waist high. Can you perceive any change in the angle of projection needed to get the greatest distance at these two different heights? To avoid waste you might carry out this experiment on a lawn that needs watering.

• *Extraneous Movement:* Try a task at which you are fairly proficient, but use your nondominant ("other") hand or foot. Do you notice any extra movement or tension in other parts of your body? Can you become more relaxed and proficient with practice?

Try a skill, such as tying your shoelace, with one hand. Do you feel tension or extra movement occurring anywhere in your body? Ask a friend to do this and observe him or her.

• *A Thought Problem:* You are running and want to change directions. Bend your knees to absorb the force and maintain your balance. In using gravity to help you "fall" in the new direction, where would you shift your center of gravity? Which way would you be leaning? Now which way would you push against the ground to go in your new direction? Try it. Does it work?

chapter five

Preparing the body to apply mechanical principles

Knowledge of the mechanical principles of movement makes us more able to utilize our bodies effectively, but we can also prepare our bodies to apply these principles more effectively. In the process of this preparation we may reap the benefits of feeling better physically, increasing the physical potential of our body structures, reducing the possibility of injuries, enhancing our responsiveness to the environment, avoiding unnecessary joint trauma, and improving or maintaining good alignment.

PREPARING THE BODY

Although sports and play can contribute very positively to the development of the body, researchers have found that our physical needs may not be totally met through specific participation and that we may need to supplement our activity program with some additional physical preparations. These may include strengthening the stabilizers of the pelvic and shoulder girdles, developing and maintaining muscle tone in the anti-gravity or postural muscles, and stretching muscles that tend to tighten (shorten).

Improving Posture. Poor posture or alignment is frequently a good indicator of your personal physical needs.

Are your shoulders forward? This could be from tight chest muscles and/or weak upper back muscles. The shoulder joint is the pivotal point around which arm movements occur. Good range of motion of this joint is necessary to allow for the time and distance needed to build force. And sufficient strength is required to stabilize this part of the body which is the foundation against which all arm movements push or pull.

Does your back sway? This could be from tight iliopsoas muscles and/or weak abdominals. The pelvic girdle is another important stabilizing area. Good abdominal development is necessary to hold the bony pelvic region in position. This stabilization is necessary for four very important mechanical functions: (1) Balance can be better controlled if the area in which the center of gravity is most frequently found can be held firmly and adjustments can be made quickly to subtle or sudden changes by the muscular control of this area. (2) The rotation of the trunk is in part carried out by the abdominal muscles. These muscles also help to hold the pelvis, allowing these trunk movements to occur. (3) All forceful moves of the legs are dependent upon a stable pelvic foundation against which to push and pull. (4) The forceful movements of the upper limbs normally originate in the pelvic region of the trunk, requiring a double stabilization—first that of the pelvic area and second that of the shoulder girdle.

Are your knees hyperextended? This could be the result of a swayback and/or tight muscles in the back of the upper legs (the hamstrings).

Do you slouch? Are you "hanging on your ligaments"? This could be caused by a lack of muscle tone in your anti-gravity or postural muscles.

Good posture or alignment is thought of as a position or positions of the body, but what actually leads to these various "good" postures is a set of important body conditions, the existence of which leads to a balance of strength and length of opposing muscle groups. If these exist one tends to have good alignment. But even more important, one has greater freedom and control to move well and readiness from which to spring into action.

Strengthening and Toning Muscles. Gravity continually pulls us toward the earth. This is evident when we are off balance and fall. To counter this pull we need muscular strength and endurance in the form of muscle tone. To prevent a fall we must contract some of our muscles to maintain our balance and then realign our center of gravity, placing ourselves in a balanced position. This is one reason why it is so important for adults to maintain strength and endurance, why children should develop strength and endurance, and why those more prone to falls and their damaging effects should enter into or continue in a developmental fitness program.

An indication of a well-conditioned muscle is *muscle tonus.* When a muscle has good tonus a number of fibers of the muscle are continuously in a state of contraction. The many fibers within the muscle share this task as a team, rotating which fibers are in contraction at any one time. This prevents fatigue and gives the muscle a feeling of firmness, while maintaining a state of continuous readiness. The "ready" condition allows an immediate adjustment to subtle or sudden changes and increases one's body control. This condition of muscle is maintained through continual healthy involvement.

Even standing and sitting require us constantly to counter the pull of gravity. If we have poor muscle tone we will tend to droop, slouch, and "hang on our ligaments," further increasing fatigue, putting stress on joint structures, and reducing our ability to make effective and rapid movement responses.

Because fitness and good alignment require maintenance of the total body some areas or muscles of the body may need specific attention to keep them effective, contributing members of the muscular system. Two areas that play a vital role in stabilization and may require additional special attention to maintain the needed strength, endurance, and muscle tone are the upper back and shoulders and the abdominals (Figure 5-1).

Observe people who droop because of poor muscle tone. Can you see why they would have more difficulty in adjusting their balance? Why would it take them longer to respond to an initial loss of balance and why would they be more apt to lose their balance and fall? Why might these people be more accident-prone and less physically skillful? Why are they less ready to move? Can you see that they have little "give" left to stop certain moves or receive force from certain directions?

Can you also see how lack of muscle tone in the upper back and shoulder muscles could result in forward, "drooping" shoulders? How weakness in the upper back and shoulder muscles could affect the preparatory backswing in a throw or racket stroke? How lack of strength in the shoulder girdle could reduce one's ability to stabilize that area to act as a brace against which a movement of the upper limb can push or pull, as in hitting or throwing?

Can you see how lack of muscle tone in the abdominals

FIGURE 5-1

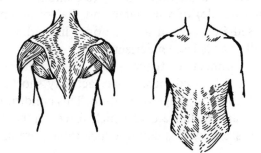

could result in a swayback? How lack of strength in the abdominals could reduce one's ability to stabilize the pelvic area, which houses the center of gravity? Keep in mind that adjusting the center of gravity plays a vital role in balance and that balance is the foundation of all movement. And remember that stabilizing the pelvis allows it to act as a brace against which a movement of the lower limb can push or pull.

Correcting Muscle Tightness. While active participants attempt to maintain adequate muscle strength and tone they may have to recognize the further need to include stretching in their fitness program to avoid muscle tightness and to ensure that an adequate range of motion (ROM) is available in the various joints of the body.

Our movement takes place around joints through a system of opposing muscles. While muscles must be strong to create and stop motion (absorb force) they must also be sufficiently long and elastic to allow for freedom of movement and a good initial position from which to move. Without periodic stretching this freedom and range of motion can be gradually diminished. (See Figure 5-2 on page 71 and 5-3 on page 72.)

Muscles that are heavily used tend to form connective tissue within them. Part of this is actually a form of scar tissue that develops as a result of the many microscopic tears or "small accidents" that normally occur during active involvement. You have probably noticed the difference in the "toughness" if you have had the opportunity to compare the chewiness of the meat (muscle) of wild game and that of an animal that has been raised in a cage or allowed only limited activity. The latter normally needs less tenderizer.

Because connective tissue shortens if not periodically stretched, a heavily used muscle may actually shorten, causing tightness and a loss in range of motion. This condition can also limit the time and distance over which force can be developed.

Can you see how this could reduce force potential, reduce

FIGURE 5-2

the "give" available in receiving a force, and increase the possibility of injuries that could lead to further tightness and joint restrictions?

This condition of tightness can pull the body out of alignment and put increased stress on the involved joints.

Within the last several years athletic coaches have begun to realize the values of stretching and have increased emphasis on stretching in their conditioning programs. Many fitness programs have also increased this component.

FIGURE 5-3

Muscles can be lengthened or their length maintained by periodic, *slow* stretching. A muscle that is or could become shortened should be brought to its full length and held on the stretch for several seconds. This should be done several times a week.

It is important to note that ballistic or forceful bounce stretching has come into question recently because of its injury potential (minor muscle tears) and the involvement of the stretch reflex, both of which can reduce the desired effect of lengthening the stretched muscle.

As shown in Figure 5-4, the four most common locations of muscle tightness tend to be the pectoralis major (upper chest

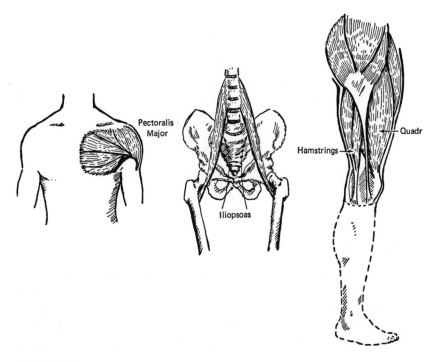

Pectoralis Major

Iliopsoas

Quadr

Hamstrings

FIGURE 5-4

and front part of the shoulder area), the iliopsoas, and the large muscles on the front (quadriceps) and the back (hamstrings) of the thighs.

The tight chest muscles (pectoralis major) pull against the upper back muscles, which may be weak, causing forward shoulders (Figure 5-5).

A tight iliopsoas pulls the vertebral column forward, and if the abdominals are not sufficiently strong to counter this pull lordosis (swayback) can result (Figure 5-6).

While the weak muscles must be strengthened their corresponding tight muscles must be lengthened. Again posture (alignment) is a good evaluation of the balance between the length and strength of opposing muscle groups.

FIGURE 5-5

Can you see how the shortening of the pectoralis major (attaching from the chest to the upper arm) could: (1) shorten upward reach? (2) limit the backswing of the arm, reducing the time and distance over which force could be developed? How the shortening of the iliopsoas muscles could: (1) pull the back

FIGURE 5-6

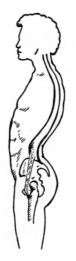

into a sway, reducing the springlike function of the curves of the vertebral column and decreasing its ability to absorb the many shocks received by the body each time one hits the ground in landing or running? (2) increase the shock trauma to the small of the back?

Can you see how tight quadriceps (found on the front of the thigh and attaching below the knee) could limit the backswing of the leg, reducing the time and distance over which force could be developed? How tight hamstrings (found on the back of the thigh and attaching below the knee) could limit the forward swing of the leg, reducing the time and distance over which force could be developed?

For a good program of strengthening and stretching discuss your needs with a physical educator or a physical fitness specialist. It might be helpful for you to learn the location and attachments of the involved muscles and the most current exercise information so that you can carefully and continuously evaluate the correctness of your exercise technique. Incorrect exercising can be harmful and can work against your efforts toward improvement.

ACTIVITIES

Specific exercises for each of these alignment problems are readily available elsewhere. I have, however, found two areas in which information seems to be limited or erroneously covered in popular sources: the lengthening of the iliopsoas and information on toe touching.

Probably the most neglected single area of possible difficulty is the stretching of the iliopsoas. Few people have ever heard of this muscle, although it contributes to countless backaches every year.

Because the iliopsoas is attached to the inside of the vertebral column in the region of the lower back (lumbar area), passes over the front of the bony pelvis, and then runs down-

ward and attaches to the inside of the upper leg bone (femur) it
is somewhat like the tight strings of a cello.

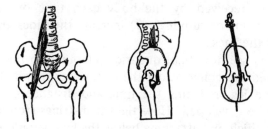

FIGURE 5-7

When this muscle shortens it pulls the small of the back forward
and down leading to a sway in the back, increasing the pressure
on the vertebral column.

Three exercises that have been used in an attempt to keep
this muscle lengthened are:

• *Flattening the small of your back while lying flat:* Try to
keep your thighs (iliopsoas attachment) on the floor while
attempting to hold your lower back on the floor. The flattening
of the back is accomplished by contracting the abdominals. The
ability to execute this exercise with ease is used as an evaluation
of the length of the iliopsoas.

FIGURE 5-8

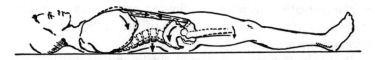

• *Lying flat on your back bring one knee to your chest
(hugging it) while you keep the other leg and the small of the
back touching the floor:* Note that the leg that is down is
the side you are actually stretching and should receive your
attention. Repeat with other leg.

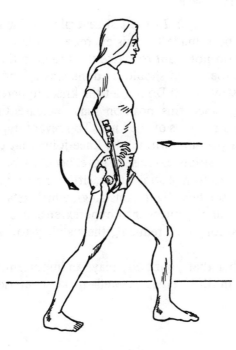

FIGURE 5-9

• *The "fencer's stretch":* Stand and place your feet in a stride position, both feet flat on the floor. The position of the back foot holds the lower attachment of the stretched iliopsoas in place. The toes of the back foot should point straight ahead. Rotate the pelvis under you pushing the upper pelvis (waist) backward while the lower pelvis rotates pressing against the iliopsoas. By pushing the upper attachment (small of the back) backward you are further stretching the iliopsoas on the back foot side. Hold this stretch for several seconds. Change stride and repeat for other side.

Because the vertebral column is so important a part of the body a medical evaluation before exercise is important.

Toe Touching.   Toe touching has long been a standard exercise for maintaining the length of the muscles in the back of the upper leg (hamstrings). In the last several years two recommendations have been made for this exercise: (1) Do not include a bounce (you do not want to evoke the stretch reflex or damage tissues). The toe touch should be done slowly and held at the point of full stretch. (2) Do not let the knees hyperextend when toe touching, since this position may increase the potential hazard to the structures of the knee. To prevent hyperextension and excessive pressure within the knee joint that can occur in the standing position exercisers have been encouraged to do their toe touches from a straight-leg, sitting position.

Can you see how tight hamstrings, which attach below the knee, could pull the knees into hyperextension or a backward "locked" position, thus reducing their ability to "give" with a force?

Remember that your body plays an important role in your involvement in life. Treat it well—make exercise a lifetime sport!

MOVING OBJECTS

part three

MOVING OBJECTS

chapter six

Rebound and roll patterns

Being able to "read an object" is an invaluable skill. Consider how this awareness could improve your ability to predict just where you should move to intercept, catch, or hit a bouncing ball or where to place a lay-up shot against the backboard in basketball. Even an initial understanding of rebound angles can help you reduce the amount of time and practice usually needed to learn this skill through trial and error. An interested eight-year-old can comprehend rebound verbally or through a drawing. You may need to encourage younger children to watch the ball and see how it bounces. This predictive ability is frequently the skill that makes success in movement activities possible or impossible. Watch an inexperienced individual struggling with the frustration that accompanies the difficulty of such experiences. A child will leave a game with a deep sense of failure or an adult will be unable to learn and enjoy the pleasures of a good game of tennis based upon this ability to make early predictions and be in the right place at the right time.

• If there were no friction between the rebounding object and the rebound surface and a very bouncy ball were utilized the rebound angle would tend to approximate the approach angle.

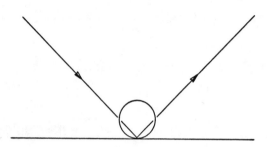

FIGURE 6-1

This friction-free rebound rarely occurs, but it does give us a point of comparison for more careful observation and the development of an awareness of the rebound patterns that can greatly improve our judgment about, effective use of, and response to the various rebounds that occur in play and sports.

DEFLECTION

Rebound is also called deflection. In the above example one of the two objects that came together was seemingly unaffected and did not move or change its position or path in space when contacted by the ball. When the weight of two objects coming together is more nearly equal both objects can be affected and deflected. In some games this double deflection and the skillful use of it are a primary aspect of the activity. Many more pins are knocked down in bowling by other pins than are knocked down by the ball. Billiards is based upon the mental skill of planning deflection and the physical skill required to execute it.

• A heavier object deflects less than a lighter object traveling at the same speed.

• The faster an object is traveling the less it will deflect.

This information must certainly be taken into account by bowlers, especially when calculating how to make a spare. You can observe the slow motion replays on television to see how deflection works for the bowler. Look at how a bowler would have to estimate the amount of deflection of the ball by how much it weighs and how fast it is traveling. Can you see why a bowling ball has an optimum (best) speed that is most effective and that if it is traveling too fast it could actually reduce the amount of "mixing" and thus the number of pins knocked down?

Can you see why heavier football players are selected for the line?

SPINS

Understanding rebound and deflection without spin establishes the foundation for understanding the complex and exciting possibilities that come about when spin is added.

• Whenever more than one force causes an effect the resulting combination of forces is known as a *resultant force.*

We have a resultant force when a spin affects the normal rebound or deflection pattern.

• When an object with spin contacts a surface the spin may give an additional "push" to the surface it contacts and may rebound in relation to this additional force.

The top-spun ball in figure 6-2 gives an extra push backward as the bottom of the ball touches the floor. Then since "to every

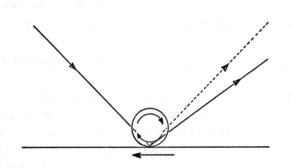

FIGURE 6-2

action there is an equal and opposite reaction" this push backward tends to send the ball forward. This additional forward force combines with the normal rebound angle and causes the ball to travel lower as it comes off the ground. Because both forces are creating a forward movement the ball will have more forward force and will thus go farther.

A spin is named according to what is occurring on the side of the ball away from the thrower (or kicker or hitter). If when viewed from the thrower's position the far side of the ball is traveling:

1. downward it is called *top spin*
2. upward it is called *backspin*
3. from left to right it is called *right spin*
4. from right to left it is called *left spin.*

A backspun ball gives an additional push *forward* against the contacted surface. The additional reaction is backwards, but as long as the forward rebound force is greater than the backward spin force the ball will still move forward. The resultant force will cause the ball to rebound higher (the attempt to go backward), and because of the two forces moving in opposite directions the ball will slow down and not go as far (Figure 6-3).

Note that only the part of the ball that touches the surface can contribute any additional push force. Thus which direction

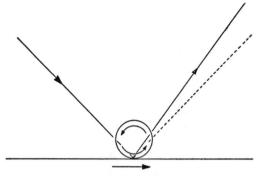

FIGURE 6-3

this part of the ball is moving on contact determines the effect. An additional consideration in left and right spin rebound patterns is which part of the contact surface has the greater effect, since the front contact surface and the back contact surface are actually moving in opposite directions. Because the back part of the contact surface is depressed more the spin direction on this part of the ball has the greatest effect with the "opposite reaction" that accompanies it. Thus a left spinning ball produces a left rebound, and so on.

We can use these resultant forces and their effects to our advantage:

1. We can confuse our opponents and make it more difficult for them to predict and thus respond effectively.
2. We can increase our control over the movement of an object so we have a broader scope of alternatives.
3. We can increase the ways we can affect other objects contacted by this spinning object.

Although the use of spins requires a greater degree of skill it does open up a whole new world of possibilities. If backspin is put on a foul shot in basketball and the ball touches the backboard, in what direction will this additional spin tend to take the ball? Is this advantageous? Is it possible that the friction created by the backspin could also slow the ball down, allowing gravity to pull it downward toward the basket?

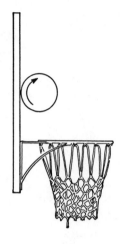

FIGURE 6-4

Why would adding a left or right spin to a lay-up shot be helpful? Which spin would you want to use? Would it be different from the other side of the basket? Would one type of spin reduce the forward force and help the ball "drop" through the basket? Would where the ball was placed on the backboard need to be different with a spin than if the ball had no spin on it? Paper and pencil may help in answering these questions.

I want my golf ball to land on the green but not to continue to roll beyond it and into a sand trap. How could I make my ball "bite" and stop?

FIGURE 6-5

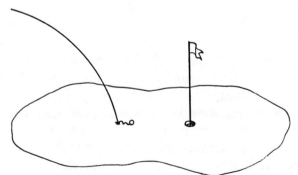

If I want my tennis ball to come up low and have additional speed what type of spin would I employ? If my opponent were deep in the court and I wanted the ball to hit and stay in the front part of the court what type of spin should I use?

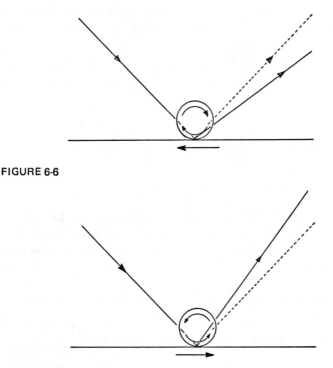

FIGURE 6-6

FIGURE 6-7

ROLL PATTERNS

As an object rolls it is affected by spins. If the part of the ball contacting the floor or ground creates an additional push as it moves along its path the object will be affected accordingly.

• We can affect the roll pattern path of a ball by adding left or right spin.

• We can affect the speed of the ball by top spin or back-spin.

• We can affect the spinning or mixing action of other objects contacted by a spinning object (as in bowling).

If a ball has backspin, as opposed to top spin, its speed will be decreased as it rolls. If a ball has top spin, as opposed to back-spin, its speed will be greater as it rolls.

If a ball has left spin on it, which way will it move as it slows down and the spin force begins to have a noticeable effect?

FIGURE 6-8

Can you see how this might allow a right-handed bowler to bring the ball into the pocket (to hit the center or "king" pin, which is the number five pin) at a sharper and more effective angle?

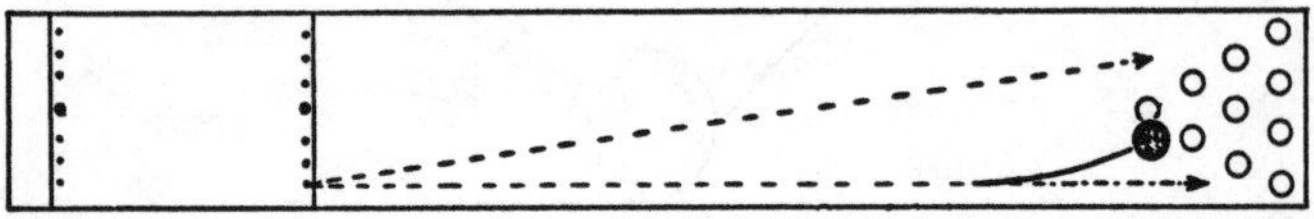

FIGURE 6-9

Figure 6-10 shows the hand position for a right-handed hook bowler. Can you see how the position of the hand in the ball creates an off-center force as the fingers leave the ball after the thumb, causing the ball to have a spin? Can you see why a left-handed and a right-handed bowler hook into the number five pin from different sides of the alley? Can you see why cutting into the center of a grouping of bowling pins with a spinning ball would have a positive effect?

FIGURE 6-10

• A spinning object will tend to impart spin to the other objects it contacts.

Can you see why this might be an advantage to "mixing" the pins in bowling?

ACTIVITIES

✓ • Encourage small children to play with balls of varying bounciness and surface textures so they will experience a variety of types of bounces and begin to be able to predict, "read," and adapt to various rebound, deflection, and roll patterns. Observe their improvement over several weeks. Their early experience is invaluable and will allow for an almost intuitive response later.

✓ • Can you bounce a ball into a box or wastepaper basket by judging the angle? If this is too difficult at first, tilt the box against the wall. Can you bounce the ball at various angles and from varying distances?

✓ • Without spin bank a ball off a wall. Hitting the same spot each time, vary your approach angle coming from the left or the right. Can you see how this change affects the rebound angle? Now mark several points along a horizontal line about shoulder high. Hitting each of these, note the angles of rebound.

✓ • Bouncing a ball on the floor, give it a hard backspin as you push it forward and downward. Can you see the effect as it hits the ground? Now do the same with top spin. Alternate left and right spin on the ball and try to determine the effect on the rebound. Remember that the back of the ball is depressed more than the front of the ball, thus the back of the ball determines the direction of the rebound.

• Throw a ball against a wall using several different types of spin. Can you differentiate the various results and clarify why these occurred? Now consider the effects of left or right spin on a normal rebound angle in a lay-up in basketball. Can you see how the approach angle might affect the rebound angle? Can you see how the point where you contact the backboard could affect the rebound angle? Can you see any advantage to adding a spin to affect the rebound angle? Can you begin to determine where you should place the ball on the backboard and what type of spin you should use to make a successful lay-up from either side of the basket?

• Using a ball, a container, and a wall can you bank a spinning ball into the container so it does not bounce back out? To become really proficient you will have to control the rebound angle and be able to "kill" the momentum of the ball. Try this experiment from both left and right sides. Note how you must reverse the spin. Can you see any relationship between this experiment and a lay-up shot? Note that the same type of spin that allows for a rebound that directs the ball more "out" toward the basket also helps reduce the momentum of the ball so that it also tends to "drop" toward the opening of the hoop.

• Find a pool table. Without spin (1) Bank the cue ball off the sides of the table. Note the resulting rebound angles. Can you begin to predict the path of the ball? As you get better at predicting the rebound angles put a "target" ball or coin on the table. Bank the cue ball in such a way that it will rebound and hit the target ball or roll over the coin. (2) Roll the cue ball into another ball. Repeat hitting the ball at various points on it. Can you begin to predict roll patterns? (3) Now put a sidespin on the ball you are rolling by spinning it like a top from above. Observe how this changes the roll pattern and the effect it has on the other balls it hits. Can you plot the difference between (2) and (3)? (4) Spin the rolled ball in the other direction. Can you plot and compare (2), (3), and (4)? Can you draw any conclusions?

• Set up two obstacles in line with each other (one behind the other). Can you roll a ball with spin so that you miss the front object and contact the object behind it? Can you do this with both a left and right spin?

Players need a great deal of experience with rebounding and roll patterns before they can respond effectively to activities that require this skill. Activities such as "Four Square"[1], bowling and pool give players the repetitive experience needed with multiple opportunities to view the way a ball moves under various conditions. All participants should be encouraged to play games that contribute to their basic skill abilities. Success in responding to any moving object is based upon either conscious or intuitive awareness. This can best be gained by a combination of thinking and experiencing.

To insure more success in play and sports we should attempt to find or create games of challenge using rebounds, deflection, and roll patterns with and without spin. Do you know of games that do this? Can you make up a fun one?

Observe various movement activities. Can you see any use of rebound, deflection, roll patterns?

---

[1] "Four Square," which involves constant evaluation of rebound angles, can be found on page 43 in *Follow Me*.

chapter seven

Projectiles

Those unaware of the mechanical principles of projectiles must learn certain skills through the arduous and frustrating process of trial and error. Many never discover the seemingly mystical flight patterns that can be effectively utilized when one understands the concepts of the parabolic path, spins, the effects of air pressure, and the role the center of gravity plays when a person becomes a projectile.

PRINCIPLES OF PROJECTILES

Knowledge of these principles will allow you to (1) determine the path of an object in flight and respond more effectively to it, and (2) select and execute flight patterns that have a specific desired result. In other words, it will give you greater control over the object and what happens to it when it lands or allow you to use it strategically to baffle an opponent. Let's look at some of these principles.

• The flight pattern of an object is normally fairly consistent. Unless modified by wind, spin, or some characteristic of the object that affects air pressure in a specific way the pattern is parabolic.

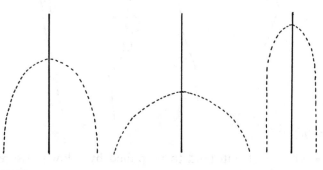

FIGURE 7-1

This simply means that the second half of the flight "mirrors" or duplicates, in reverse, the first half of the pattern. Being aware of this may help those receiving an object to determine the path it will take and where it will come down. Thus they become more able to "read" the flight of an object.

The exception to the parabolic flight principle that we experience most frequently in sports involves a spinning object. We can affect the normal flight pattern by creating an off-center force on the projected object, thus causing the object to rotate. This in turn creates an uneven air pressure system around the outside of the object (Figure 7-2).

• A spinning object will "pull" air molecules around its surface as it spins.

When air molecules collide a high-pressure area forms. A spinning object can also help pull air around its surface and thus create low-pressure areas.

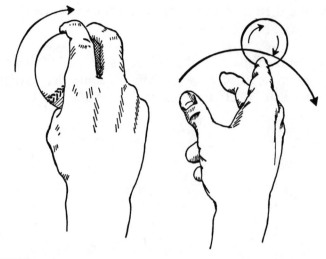

FIGURE 7-2

• An object will tend to be pulled by a low-pressure area (suction) and pushed by a high-pressure area, thus causing the object to move in the direction of a low-pressure area.

This applies to all spins whether they be left, right, top, back or diagonal spins. Figure 7-3 would be a backspin ball and this ball will tend to lift as it travels through the air, because of the high-pressure "collision" area that will occur at the front bottom of the ball while a low-pressure (suction) area forms as the air at the upper front of the ball is pulled from that area.

FIGURE 7-3

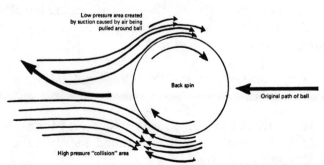

Low pressure area created by suction caused by air being pulled around ball

Back spin

Original path of ball

High pressure "collision" area

The following spins will have the following effects on the path of a round object:

1. In a top spin the ball will go down.
2. In a backspin the ball will go up.
3. In a left spin the ball will go left.
4. In a right spin the ball will go right.
5. In diagonal spin that mixes top spin and right spin the ball will go right and down.
6. In a diagonal spin that mixes backspin and left spin the ball will go left and up.

Could you mix other combinations and determine where the ball will go? If you wanted the ball to dive would you be able to determine what type of spin to apply? Can you think of three specific situations in which spins would be advantageous?

The surface of the object can also affect how much air is pulled around the object. A golf ball has dimples. This gives little pockets to carry additional air to the back of the ball, helping to prevent a vacuum from forming, which might reduce the forward momentum of the ball and cause it to move in an unpredictable flight pattern.

Can you see why a new fuzzy tennis ball may have more spin effect than a balding one? Can you see why a major league umpire examines a foul tipped ball so carefully before it is allowed to be returned to play?

HOW TO APPLY SPIN TO AN OBJECT

An object can be made to rotate by applying an off-center force to it. Off-center refers to a force that is not applied directly through the center of an object.

This can be accomplished by striking the object off center (as in tennis, golf, or volleyball), by using holes (as a hook delivery in bowling), or by using seams (as with a curve ball pitch in baseball) to put additional force on one side of the ball. (See chapter 6 for examples of other situations where spin can be helpful.)

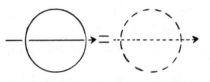

FIGURE 7-4

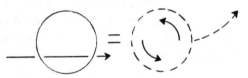

FIGURE 7-5

It is important to remember that there are situations in which a mishap can cause an unwanted spin, such as the slice or hook in golf. These can be eliminated by correcting whatever is causing the object to spin. Perhaps you have already heard the admonitions "Hit *through* the *center* of the ball" or "Draw your racket *through* the ball."

THE HUMAN BODY AS A PROJECTILE

The body becomes a projectile whenever it leaves the ground. And our center of gravity does follow a parabolic path. But because we can change the position of the center of gravity within the body we can do some interesting things to affect our body position during flight and landing (Figure 7-6).

• Once your body leaves the ground the path of the center of gravity cannot be changed.

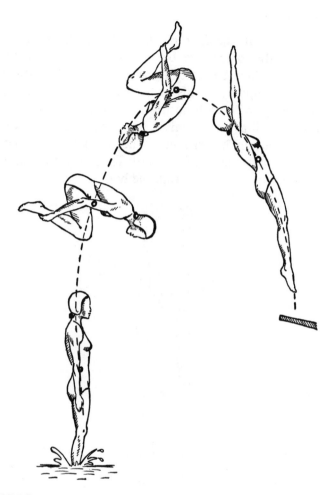

FIGURE 7-6

• You can, however, modify your body parts around your center of gravity while you are in the air.

• When you change the position of any body part the center of gravity shifts within the body to the new center of weight distribution. The parabolic path of the center of gravity does not, however, change.

Before we can put these ideas together for effective use each of these concepts must be clearly and separately understood.

In a normal standing position the center of gravity is located roughly somewhere behind the umbilicus (belly button). Each individual's center of gravity would be slightly different depending upon how his or her weight is distributed. This will also change with each position in which a person places his or her body. If a person raises her arms over her head her weight distribution has changed. The point that balances the weight evenly must also shift upward. Thus raising the arms also raises the center of gravity within the body.

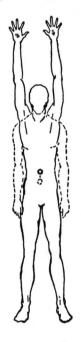

FIGURE 7-7

If a person lifts an arm or leg to the side, the center of gravity will shift in *that* direction to divide evenly the new weight distribution. Remember, *any positional change of the body relocates the center of gravity within the body.* But keep in mind that the parabolic path of the center of gravity cannot be altered once the body has left the ground and become a projectile.

Before you begin to apply the combination of these principles to a human body flight let's review the last concept.

If you reposition your weight in any direction by moving a body part (arms, legs, head, bend the trunk) your center of gravity will also shift *in that direction* within the body to divide the newly distributed weight. For instance, if you lift your leg to the right your center of gravity will shift up and to the right within your body to become your new center of weight distribution. Although you can change the position of the center of gravity within your body during flight by changing the position of your body parts you cannot change the flight path of the center of gravity once your body is airborne.

So, body position in air will change in relation to the new weight distribution while the center of gravity of the body retains its original parabolic flight pattern.

If my center of gravity shifts upward in my body because I raise my arms but the path of my center of gravity cannot change, then the position of my feet in air will be lower than before I raised my arms.

FIGURE 7-8

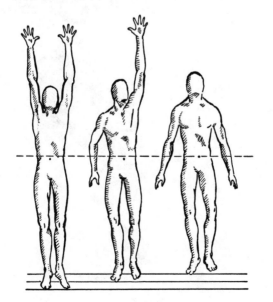

The opposite also holds true. If I lower my arms during flight the position of my feet should be higher than if I did not lower them. Timing will be important in utilizing this possibility effectively. This poses some interesting questions:

- Should I raise one or both arms in a jump and reach activity?
- When I am going for height should both legs be in a downward position at the height of the jump (lay-up, dunk shot, spike in volleyball)?

FIGURE 7-9

• Remembering that the parabolic path of the center of gravity does not change once the body is in flight, could I put my feet farther *forward* in a broad jump by having my arms back just *before* landing (causing my center of gravity to be farther backward in my body and my legs to be farther forward than if both my arms and legs were forward)? I would still need to bring my arms forward upon landing to bring the center of gravity forward in my body so I would not lose my balance backward.

• At the highest point of a dive would I be able to get the appearance of more height or "hang" in air if I piked my dive?

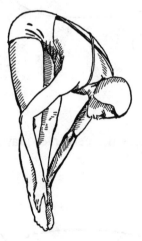

FIGURE 7-10

Now these same principles also become important if you are attempting to clear an obstacle, such as a hurdle, a high jump, or a pole vault bar or if you are vaulting some object. Perhaps a historical example of the changing high jump technique would help make this possibility more clear. Over the years three basic and distinct techniques have evolved. Each has brought new height records.

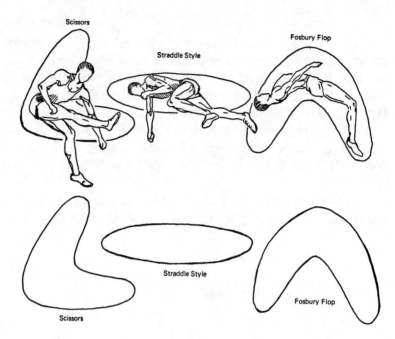

FIGURE 7-11

Now let's approximate the center of gravity (•) in relation to each of these shapes.

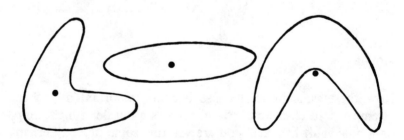

FIGURE 7-12

Now let's draw in high jump bars at the height at which they can be cleared by each of the specific high jump techniques (using the same center of gravity path).

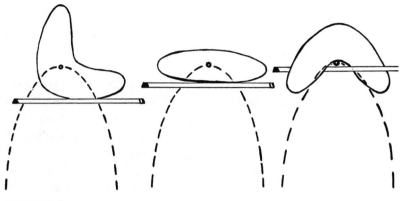

FIGURE 7-13

Scissors: In the scissors technique, the high position of the upper trunk plus the lifting of both legs raises the center of gravity fairly high in the body. This places a great deal of body mass between the center of gravity and the bar.

Straddle Style: Because the body is laid out horizontally in straddle style there is not as much body mass to have to pass between the center of gravity and the bar.

Fosbury Flop: In the Fosbury flop technique the center of gravity is actually outside the body. The flop takes the upper trunk over first. As the upper body clears the bar it is quickly lowered (lowering the center of gravity within the body) and you can almost see the lift of the body.

Can you see how these evolving techniques have used the concept of repositioning the body while in flight to shift the position of the center of gravity in relation to the body, thus helping to lift various body parts higher and decreasing the possibility of the body interfering with the bar?

• Newton's Action/Reaction principle: "To every action there is an equal and opposite reaction" is also involved in changing the position of the body in flight. If one body part is moved a counterforce will be exerted on another body part. If an action occurs above the center of gravity it should produce a reaction below the center of gravity.

Thus, if an arm or the head is dropped another body part may rise. In the Fosbury flop the legs will lift, helping them to clear the bar as the head and shoulders are dropped downward after passing over the bar. This general concept can be applied to various positional changes in the body while in flight.

Of course the technique used in each of the high jumps discussed becomes progressively more sophisticated, and without skill the risk of injury also increases. For this reason it is wise to start beginners with the simpler techniques.

In hurdling, should I try to lean my trunk forward over the hurdle rather than leaving my trunk in a more upright position? Why or why not? (Relate to the center of gravity and body position and the action/reaction counterforce effect.)

FIGURE 7-14

Would it be helpful to bring my lead leg down quickly, thus "stepping" the hurdle? Does this have anything to do with the body-center of gravity relationship or the action/reaction counterforce effect?

FIGURE 7-15

Observe sports events in which humans are projectiles. Can you begin to see situations in which the principles we have been discussing could possibly by applied?

OBSERVATIONS AND ACTIVITIES

• *Jump and reach:* Attempt to touch something above you. Make sure it is safe before you try. First reach with both hands. Then reach with one hand. Then reach with one hand while bringing the other arm down to your side. (For some this may feel awkward and distracting at first and may actually reduce the height of your initial attempts.)

After these three forms of jumping became comfortable, were there any measurable differences or improvements?

• Jump and reach with the "lifting" leg staying in the up position; then jump and reach with the "lifting" leg being brought down just before the height of the jump is reached. (Timing may be difficult.)

Was there any measurable difference?

Can you devise experiments to test these principles? Remember that the center of gravity is also a vital component of balance. If you are not able to bring your center of gravity over your base of support upon landing you will be faced with the additional problems created by loss of balance. You may want to think about how you absorb force.

chapter eight

Direction and accuracy

Skill is frequently the combination of the development of a given amount of force and the ability to apply this force in a specific direction. To be successful at many tasks it is important to understand how to affect direction. With this knowledge it is not only possible to determine how and why to do something but it is also possible to find the cause of and solution to undesirable results.

For example, if a tennis serve that is taken on a full reach and has good force behind it is going into the net or hitting beyond the service area, this is a directional problem, not a force problem, and it is possible to analyze from the results that the contact point on the ball and the angle of the racket face may need to be changed to correct for this (Figure 8-1).

By moving the ball toss slightly forward when the serve is going beyond the service area and backward if the ball is going into the net the contact points and the racket angles become

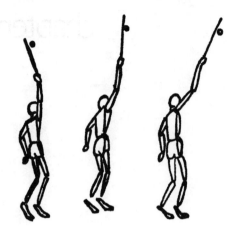

FIGURE 8-1

FIGURE 8-2

more appropriate and the serve can be directed more accurately (Figure 8-2). Can you see how the contact point in the under-hand serve in volleyball is affected by the position the ball is held for the serve (Figure 8-3)?

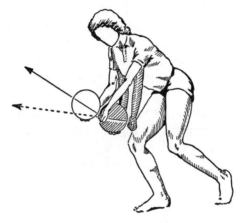

FIGURE 8-3

Can you see how this relates to the previous analysis?

Direction and accuracy are related to the skills of throwing, rebounding, moving, striking, deflection, and so on. Some factors affecting direction and accuracy apply to all of these while others apply only to certain of these skills. As you read and participate attempt to recognize which factors can be related to which skills. It is a challenge to take information and make it work for you and others. And you must realize that there are no simple answers for all situations but that *you* have to determine all the factors in any given situation and select the most appropriate solutions. As the situation changes, and it will, you will need to reevaluate and determine new possibilities.

FACTORS THAT AFFECT DIRECTION
AND ACCURACY

The Pull of Gravity. Gravity constantly pulls all things toward the earth. Thus gravity has a directional effect that we can put to use. By putting just the right amount of force on the basketball or golf ball we can control its "drop" through the basket or onto the green. We can hit a Texas Leaguer in baseball or softball, execute a dropshot or a well-placed lob in tennis, or cast a plug or fly into the chosen spot in fishing. These skills reflect the ability to compare, contrast, and control the various paths that result from varying amounts of force applied in projecting an object.

Experience allows us to become increasingly intuitive and skillful about receiving and projecting objects. This can be translated into a growing ability to "read" and control one's environment, which can be important in life situations other than sport and play.

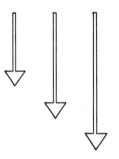

FIGURE 8-4

Air Resistance. Air resistance can affect direction in three ways:

1. Wind or drafts may be a factor. Sometimes you must reduce their negative effect and on other occasions you can actually use them to your advantage. Have you ever seen a punter who utilized the wind? Wind can be so helpful that rules are written into track and

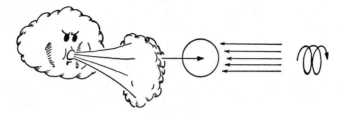

FIGURE 8-5

field regulations prohibiting the establishment of records if the wind direction and speed are too advantageous.

2. Light objects with proportionally large surface areas are affected by air resistance to a much greater extent than heavy objects with a relatively small surface. We see this in the flight patterns of balloons and badminton birds. A badminton bird does not move in a parabolic pattern since the direction of its flight is affected by air resistance.

FIGURE 8-6

3. The various air pressures created by spins can also affect the direction of the flight of an object. Note the section on spins in chapter 6.

Timing and Flattening the Swinging Arc. The term *swinging* arc refers to the path (arc) made by the body part (hand, foot) or striking implement (bat, racket, club).

FIGURE 8-7

To see the arc pattern the viewer needs to be parallel to the swing. In a ground stroke in tennis or batting in baseball or softball one would have to view it from above.

FIGURE 8-8

In golf, pitching, or a foot pass in soccer one could best see the arc while facing the player.

FIGURE 8-9

These views place you parallel or horizontal to the movement and allow you a better view of the flattening of the swinging arc.

Many inexperienced participants have difficulty with placement of a throw or hit because they tend to swing in a somewhat circular arc rather than flattening the arc as much as possible. Since an object will tend to travel in the direction of the applied force from the point of release or impact a circular arc that creates a continuously changing directional pattern makes accuracy more difficult. In these circumstances accuracy is based upon the almost perfect timing of the release or contact, which is extremely difficult to achieve, especially for the beginner.

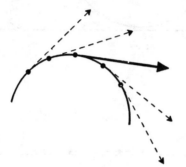

FIGURE 8-10

If, however, the arc of the swinging arm, leg, or striking implement can be flattened, the release or impact can occur at any of several points during the swing since the direction of applied force remains the same over an extended period of the swing.

FIGURE 8-11

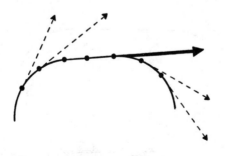

Can you see how this could be important in golf, a foot pass in soccer, a drive in hockey, pitching, kicking, throwing, batting, racket strokes, and even bowling?

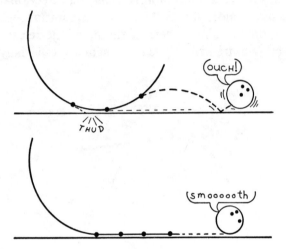

FIGURE 8-12

It is important to remember that the swinging arc can be flattened by four basic techniques: transferring weight, leading with sequential body parts, moving forward over a bent forward knee, and reaching out during the follow-through.

Transferring weight: In transferring the weight we begin swinging around one pivotal point and as the weight is shifted we are actually swinging around a second pivotal point, which creates a flattened arc.

FIGURE 8-13

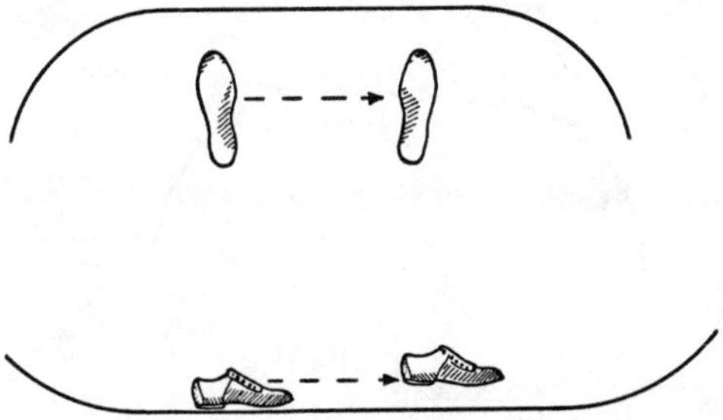

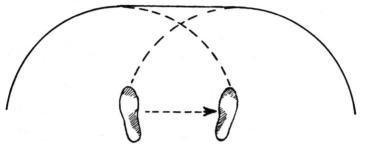

FIGURE 8-14

Leading with sequential body parts: Observe a baseball batter, a slow motion throw, a tennis player stroking a ground stroke or a golfer hitting a drive. Can you see the hips leading, then the shoulder? This lead moves to the next joint and then on to the next joint. It takes a keen eye and careful observations to see this technique.

Moving forward over a bent forward knee: The arc will be flattened by (1) keeping the body moving in one plane; (2) encouraging a greater transfer of weight; and (3) keeping the center of gravity lower and over the base of support, improving one's balance potential. Remember, a loss of balance, even a slight wobble, can affect accuracy and direction.

Reaching out in the desired direction during the follow-through: Reaching out contributes to the continued flattening of the swinging arc. Concentration on following through in the desired direction is vital. Its contribution to both flattening the arc and the level swing of the impact force is very important. A complete follow-through also plays a major role in insuring that slowing down does not occur during the force development stage.

Direction of Impact Force. An object will accelerate in the direction of the force of impact.

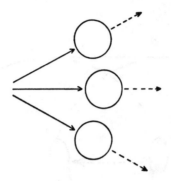

FIGURE 8-15

If the direction of impact force is a "scoop" or "chop" the resulting path of the object will be considerably different than if the direction of impact is level.

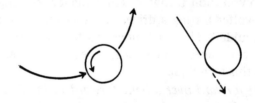

FIGURE 8-16

If the direction of impact does not pass directly through the center of gravity of the object being struck a spin will occur and its effects will contribute to the resultant direction. (Note the section on spins in chapter 6.)

Contact Point. If the direction of the impact force passes through the center of gravity of the object being struck the contact point can become an instructional focal point.

Here again we are dealing with an equal and opposite reaction. An awareness that if you hit under an object it will go up and if an object goes up you have hit under it should help a player to avoid repeating ineffective actions and applications of force. This can then be applied to all directions, down, right, left, and so on.

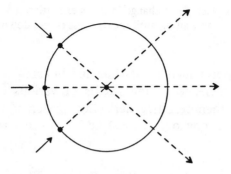

FIGURE 8-17

Perhaps the contact point on the object is one of the most effective points of concentration for many participants. It gives a relatively clear and specific single point of reference while other related factors of kinesthetic awareness (feeling and sensing the position of your body without visual assistance) or the difficult task of evaluating a moving striking implement may be too complex for many.

To modify the contact point a player has several options:

1. reposition the object (as in a volleyball or tennis serve)
2. reposition oneself in relation to the object (as in golf)
3. focus and concentrate on the desired point of contact (as in striking by batting, kicking, or racket strokes)
4. check to see if one is utilizing the techniques that flatten the arc
5. change one's timing (either meet the ball sooner or later in the swing, as shown in Figure 8-18)

FIGURE 8-18

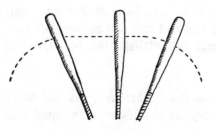

6. check the need for a change in one's execution. (Are you swinging level? Are you waiting until the ball toss comes down too low on the tennis serve?)

Deflection sports such as bowling and billiards depend upon a thorough knowledge of the results of various contact point impacts and their resulting deflection patterns. This is especially true when one object must be hit in order to hit another object.

Angle of Rebound or Striking Surface. The angle of the rebound or striking surface (the direction in which the surface is facing) affects the rebound direction of an object hitting this surface. This is true whatever the surface is: wall, floor, racket, club, hand, or foot.

FIGURE 8-19

Can you relate the angle of the rebound or striking surface to various sports? For instance, hitting in billiards, pool, golf, or baseball? Wall or ceiling shots in racketball, handball, or squash? Backboard shots and bounce passes in basketball? Can you see this principle applied in blocked shots like a net volley or a half volley in tennis? A spike in volleyball or a trap in soccer? Can you judge the angle of the ball coming off the ground (bouncing) in baseball or softball, tennis, racketball, handball, or squash?

The Action/Reaction Principle. As we have previously discussed "to every action there is an equal and opposite reaction." If you wish to run, walk, or swim forward then whenever possible all your push or pull should be in a backward direction. Any push or pull not in line with and opposite to the desired reaction can lead to less desirable results. Can you see how toeing out or in could lead to wasted effort? Could you analyze the effects of various swimming strokes in relation to this principle?

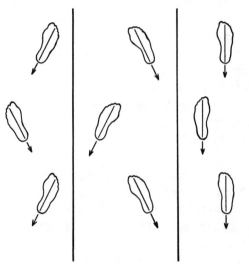

FIGURE 8-20

Can you see how the action/reaction principle also relates to angles of rebound, contact points, direction of impact force, flattening of the swinging arc, and timing of the release or striking point?

Resultant Force. Forces are frequently found working in combination with other forces. Only occasionally will a single force be in operation in a given situation. When forces work together we have what is known as a resultant force and in turn have a resultant effect.

An example might be a racket contacting a ball in which the result may be affected by:

1. the direction of the impact force of the striking implement
2. the point of contact
3. the angle of the rebound surface
4. any spin on the ball at the time of impact.

Figuring out resultant forces and their effects can be fun and challenging. It is perhaps easiest to begin by determining the additional effect that each would contribute and how this would change the usual result. We have already done this in part by observing the effects of spins on the normal rebound pattern.

Understanding and predicting possible effects of various factors on direction may help you alter your techniques. This will become more essential as you seek to become highly skilled or to coach the skillful player.

The Participant's Body. Four factors that can negatively affect our ability to execute directional control are: (1) inability to stabilize or set body parts that create a foundation against which moving parts can push or pull; (2) lack of good balance (the foundation from which we direct force); (3) excessive tension, which can inhibit our ability to execute appropriate techniques; and (4) extraneous (unnecessary) movements, which may contaminate directional application of force.

OBSERVATIONS AND ACTIVITIES

• Observe the effect of gravity. Push or toss a ball into the air. Watch it carefully. Can you see how it slows down as it rises and pauses slightly at the peak of the toss? As the ball moves downward the speed with which it is traveling is increased by the continuous pull of gravity. At what point would a beginner find the ball easiest to contact in relation to the speed at which it is moving? Can you relate this to a tennis serve?

• Loft several paper wad balls into a basket several feet away. Are you (almost without being aware of it) developing a technique based upon the pattern of the pull of gravity?

• Note your follow-through when you throw a ball. Are you swinging your hand and arm directly out toward the basket? This insures a good direction of flight. Observe others' follow-through. Observe the follow-through in kicking and striking activities. Can you see why the follow-through in shooting activities, such as archery or riflery, is a "hold" or "freeze" in the final position and is absolutely vital to accuracy?

• Taking a light ball, such as a beach ball, whiffle ball, or table tennis ball, attempt to spin it in various directions as you throw it forward. Can you observe the various flight patterns in relation to the different spins? Can you explain why each of these occur?

• Practice leading with each sequential body part as described in chapter 4. Can you see why this affects the direction of a projectile?

• Place a four-foot length of plain shelf paper on a table. Facing the table, grip a marking pen so that you can draw the path of your hand as it passes along the table. Attempt to flatten your moving hand and arm as you do the following:

1. transfer your weight from your back foot to your front foot as you move your arm forward
2. repeat without any weight transfer
3. lead with each sequential body part
4. repeat, keeping joints straight; don't lead
5. have your forward knee bent as you move your weight forward
6. repeat, keeping your knee straight as you move forward
7. try reaching out on the follow-through
8. repeat, but do not reach out on the follow-through.

Can you see the effect on the flattening of the arc as you attempt each of these? If you have had difficulty differentiating the various trials you might use different colored marking pens.

• If you can go to a bowling lane observe the path of the ball of a proficient bowler.

Note how the arc is flattened by getting down over a bent knee, transferring the weight forward, and reaching out on the follow-through. Try it.

Attempt to find a bowler who drops or bounces the ball onto the alley. Can you diagnose why this occurs? Can you see why a smooth bowling release would have greater consistency and thus greater accuracy?

Observe a hook ball roll. Can you determine how the hand position puts spin on the ball even without any turning of the hand? Can you see why trying to put spin on a hook delivery by twisting the hand or lifting the wrist might prove ineffective for the beginner or inexperienced bowler?

• Tee a ball (Figure 8-21). You might also choose to hang a tarp or heavy cloth to hit into. This could be marked with target areas.

FIGURE 8-21

Using various directions of impact, including "chopping" and "scooping" actions, hit the ball off the tee. Note the effect on the ball. Now practice hitting with a level (horizontal to the ground) swing. Each time the ball rises more than you want it to, what should you check about your swing? What if the ball goes down? What if it goes left or right? Can you see how this latter problem involves the flattening of the swinging arc rather than the levelness of the swing to the ground? Can you separate these two problems and see how they differ?

Hit the teed ball at several different contact points. Can you see how this affects the direction the ball takes? Can you reverse your analysis and go from result to cause (for instance, the ball went up, thus it must have been hit from below).

Hit the ball off center. The result should be a spin. Can you determine the type of spin imparted and the directional effect of each type of spin?

• Can you find a means by which you can alter the angle of a rebound surface? Changing the angle of the rebound surface, experiment and observe results. Can you predict results? When would this information be important?

• Take a pole that has sufficient length yet is light enough that you can hold it up high without excessive fatigue. An old bamboo fishing pole works well. Tie a string or fishing line to it and to the free end of the string attach a paper clip. Now place the plastic part of a badminton shuttlecock in the clip as shown.

FIGURE 8-22

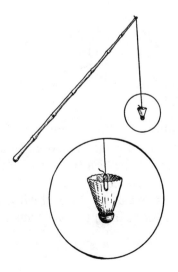

Have the bird held at three different points: out in front of you approximately one and a half to two feet, directly over your head, and slightly behind you.

FIGURE 8-23

The bird should be held high enough to force you to take a *full* reach as you hit it from each position. Note the direction of flight, contact point on the bird (under, behind, above) and the angle of the striking surface. To accomplish the latter you may have to hold your racket up to the bird without striking it. Can you draw any conclusions from this experiment?

Note: If you must work alone tie the line or string overhead then place yourself in various positions under the bird.

Can you relate this experiment to: (1) a tennis serve, (2) an overhead volleyball serve, (3) an underhand volleyball serve, (4) a spike in volleyball, (5) a golf drive, (6) a smash in tennis or badminton, (7) a *low* short serve in badminton, (8) a drop shot in badminton?

I want to hit my golf drive lower. According to the above which direction would I move to accomplish this? I want to hit a ball to right field; at what point in its flight should I attempt to hit the ball?

- Predict the movement patterns in the following figures.

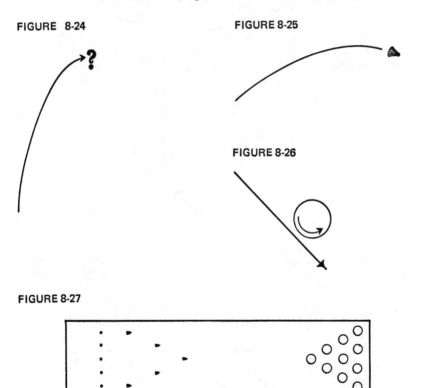

FIGURE 8-24

FIGURE 8-25

FIGURE 8-26

FIGURE 8-27

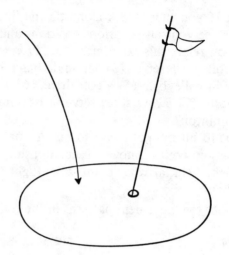

FIGURE 8-28

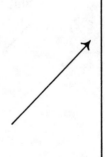

FIGURE 8-29

FIGURE 8-30

Remembering that a left or right spin is named by what is happening to the front of the ball, try to identify and predict the movement patterns in figures 8-31 and 8-32.

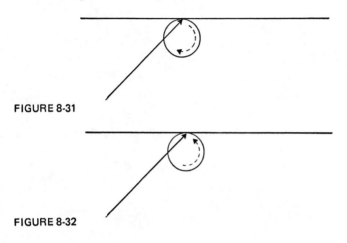

FIGURE 8-31

FIGURE 8-32

part four

IMPROVING ANALYTICAL SKILLS

chapter nine

Visual
evaluation

Good visual evaluation can be extremely helpful. It can assist you to predict what will happen and allow you to be ready for it. I have found good visual evaluation second only to good balance in successful sports and play.

For beginners it is important to learn to "keep your eye on the ball." Intermediate players need to become proficient at evaluating the path of the ball, assessing its travel speed, and making visual estimations of distance. They must also learn to judge and predict rebounds (including bounces) and begin to "read" the movements of an opponent. Advanced players become sensitive to early indicators that will help them determine and adjust to unusual conditions, make effective predictions that will allow them to be where the action is, and at a quick glance "read" an entire situation to make important split second decisions. These skills are developmental and require experience. But being aware of the basic principles in chapters 6, 7, and 8 and involving carefully selected and related experiences can help to reduce the time required to gain and improve these skills.

EVALUATION SKILLS
AND HOW TO IMPROVE THEM

Some of the specific visual skills that can be developed or improved are:

1. visual concentration
2. visual tracking—the ability to follow the movement of an object or person over time
3. reading and predicting movement of an object, of an opponent, or of a situation
4. visual figure/ground discrimination—the ability to separate the relevant (figure) from the competing irrelevant stimuli (ground)
5. relating and evaluating multiple visual stimuli simultaneously.

Visual evaluation can be improved with practice, especially if that practice is planned to be specifically enriching and instructive. For example, individuals must be able to concentrate their focus on an object to track it visually as it travels through space. Without the former skill the latter becomes much more difficult and may remain weak. Concentrating one's focus first on a still object, then on one that is moving slowly and in a predetermined pattern can progressively improve the set of skills required to track a free-flying object at various speeds and variable patterns.

Following are some suggestions, but be analytical and inventive yourself. You may discover methods and techniques that are even more helpful.

• Tee an object on a holding device of some sort and let the player hit it.

• Tether or tie an object. First allow a player to hit the ball while it is still. As success increases, add a challenge by swinging the ball ever so slightly in line with the swinging pattern of the hitter. Then allow the player to see how many times in a row he or she can hit the swinging object. You can also tether an object with a clip device (or the creative use of Velcro) so that a solid contact will release the object and hitters can see the results of their concentration and tracking. If contacting the moving object is difficult have the individual work on improving visual concentration and focus first. One way to do this is to mark the tethered ball with letters, colors, or words. Then, giving a very slow spin to the swinging object, ask the player to attempt to identify or read in sequence what is on the ball.

Remember, skills are developmental and our task is to find what aspect or aspects need help and how we can creatively and effectively extend the needed help. A player's optimal ability may never be reached if the foundation skills are left incompletely developed or are neglected because the player can hit or catch a ball and is having some success. We need to find enjoyable activities to give each participant challenging experiences that allow for continuous growth and development.

Rebound devices are available that allow practice catching by oneself when another player is not available. The side of a building or a set of steps has served this purpose for almost as long as there have been walls and balls.

John Kelly, an ingenious and creative Philadelphian, developed a large pinball-type box that allows a child to toss a ball up into it, watch it change direction several times, and predict where it will drop out of the end of the device. By involving a few removable parts he is able to make the path of the ball consistent, irregular, simple, or complex. An adjustable tilt-angle of the box allows some control of the speed of the ball.

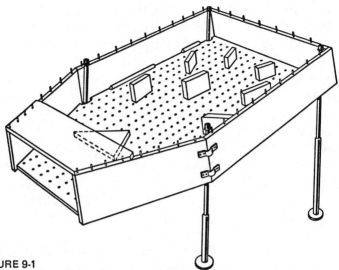

FIGURE 9-1

You may want to change the size or color of the object to assist the individual who is having difficulty. Perhaps the object is traveling too fast. Playing with a beach ball or balloon may help. Juggling certainly encourages continuous improvement of visual concentration and tracking and can be a challenge to the more highly skilled player.

Another important skill related to visual evaluation is the ability to "read" movement patterns, to gain early cues, and thus to be able to predict and respond more successfully. This could involve predicting where an object will land, how fast it is traveling, the angle at which it will rebound, where another player is, what that player's next move might be, whether an opponent has put a spin on the ball, and how will the flight and rebound be affected by various conditions.

OBSERVATIONS AND ACTIVITIES

• Begin with slow "mirroring" or "shadowing." This is a process where one individual or a group attempts to follow and duplicate all the movements of another.

134

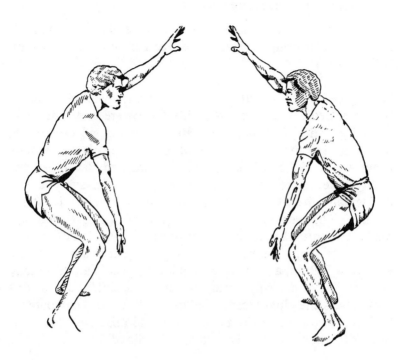

FIGURE 9-2

• To increase the challenge, simulate a basketball guarding situation in which there are stops, starts, and an attempt to lose a guard.

• A good game to try is *Team Juggle*.[1] Using soft objects such as yarn balls, large paper wads wrapped with a rubber band, sock balls, small pillows, etc., have players attempt to keep as many of these objects moving through the air at one time as they can. The thrower is responsible for helping the receiver make a good catch. If an object falls to the ground anyone can pick it up and start it again. (Be careful not to bump heads when picking up an object.) You must get the receiver's attention *before* you can throw an object to them.

[1] This game can be found in *Follow Me.*

- A balloon with some beans or water in it will tend to move irregularly and simulate the free ball movement in football.

Many seeing a skillful player making a well-coordinated response credit it to "natural ability," unaware of the developmental practice that built this ability to respond effectively. Some also see these skills as useful only during play. But many times we could avoid an accident if we had developed the ability to evaluate visually, adapt, and respond. Have you ever accidentally dropped something and caught it before it hit the ground? The person who can make good visual evaluations might be more able to avoid collision in a possible automobile accident or simply be better able to park a car in a small space. Robert W. White, a Harvard psychologist, once said, "Play may be fun, but it is also a serious business in childhood. During these hours the child steadily builds up his (or her) competence in dealing with the environment." I would raise only one question: Why should this be limited to "childhood"?

Play may be the key to open many doors to lifelong growth and development. Understanding seems to lead to further understanding and gradually you are actually playing with the secrets to success in sport and play. For some of you the enjoyment of learning can become play in itself as you help yourself and others move well. Hopefully the reading of this book and your participation in the activities described have been a pleasurable experience encouraging you to continue to choose play as a lifelong involvement.

appendix

Putting it all together: some suggestions on striking

- *Relax* so you can get a free and easy *full* swing. This will not only add force but will make the path of your swing more consistent.

- *Keep your eye on the object to be struck.*

- *Predict the path of the object.* (Know the effects of gravity, air resistance, spins, and rebounds.) Don't wait for the ball to get to you before beginning to determine its path.

- *Swing level* or in line with the path of the object to be struck so you can meet the ball at any of several points along its path.

- If you need *force*:

1. use a long lever (that you can still control)
2. study factors that help you overcome inertia
3. take a complete backswing
4. involve the stretch reflex

5. be sure to involve all contributing body parts, including trunk rotation (use opposition)
6. add body parts sequentially from center of gravity out to the end of the involved levers
7. be careful that you do not "give" on impact
8. transfer weight in desired direction
9. follow through
10. increase the time and distance over which your force is developed.

- If you need *accuracy:*

1. shorten the lever for greater control
2. flatten the swinging arc
3. be sure your swing and follow-through are in the desired direction
4. understand the effects of contact point, direction of impact force, angle of impact surface, spin, and other contributing factors.

- If you need *speed of rotation* of the striking implement to get quickly to the object to be struck:

1. shorten the striking lever
2. shorten the preliminary actions (reduce or eliminate the backswing).

Index

NOW . . . Announcing Another Fine Book by Marianne Torbert

FOLLOW ME: A Handbook of Movement Activities for Children
Play can be fun, but it is also a time when children develop a view of themselves, of others, and the world around them. With over 100 movement activities that help children feel a sense of personal success, FOLLOW ME helps children develop self-control, muscular control, and specific perceptual motor skills while increasing their attention span and concentration. FOLLOW ME, published in 1980, has been highly acclaimed by parents and educators as a book which successfully shows the potential of play and has shown us the way to play with a purpose.

322891 $5.95   1980   224 pages

To order FOLLOW ME, please complete the form below.

Please send me _____ copies of *Follow Me* by Marianne Torbert (322891)
Enclosed is my check or money order for   _____

_____ Yes, please send me the Spectrum Catalog of all your fine books.   ___.50
Please add 50ᶜ per book for postage and handling.   _____

TOTAL   _____

Name   _____

Address   _____

City   _____ State _____ Zip _____

Cut out and mail this form to: Prentice-Hall, Inc.
                                Spectrum Books
                                Att: C. Moffa
                                Englewood Cliffs, New Jersey 07632

Prices subject to change without notice. Please allow 4 weeks for delivery.

Also Available From Marianne Torbert is a test program to use with SECRETS TO SUCCESS IN SPORT & PLAY. You can obtain a copy by writing to Marianne Torbert, Physical Education, Temple University, Philadelphia, Pennsylvania 19122.

SECRETS TO SUCCESS IN SPORT AND PLAY
A Guide for Players of All Ages
Marianne Torbert

This guide shows how young and old sports participants can improve their physical coordination, enjoy sports more, and develop skills they can transfer from sport to sport. In addition to scores of practical and challenging exercises, SECRETS TO SUCCESS IN SPORT AND PLAY tells readers how to transfer their ability from sport to sport • how to increase flexibility and reduce injuries • how to improve visual perception and accuracy • how to improve their balance • and more.